Deer on a Tote Road

Deer on a Tote Road

Written by Yvonne Joseph

Deer on a Tote Road

Copyright © 2022 Yvonne Joseph

All rights reserved. No part of this book may be reproduced or used in any manner without prior written permission of the copyright owner, except for the use of brief quotations in a book review. This book was created from my personal diaries. All names within the book are fictitious or coincidental to protect the privacy of all parties. Please note that I have taken liberties with the dates to protect all involved as well.

To request permissions, please contact the author at
yvonnejosephauthor@gmail.com

Paperback ISBN: 978-1-7366000-4-7

Ebook ISBN: 978-1-7366000-5-4

First Paperback Edition

MSB Publishing Company
Published in the United States of America

Deer on a Tote Road

Dedication

This book is dedicated to my hard-working husband, Nick. Beyond all else, he is a survivor. He has lived through the unimaginable and never stopped working to support our family and our dreams. I can never thank him enough for the life that we have.

A special thank you to our daughter, Kenzie. She is now a grown woman who reminds me every day that we can do anything we set our minds to. Her strength and independence are an inspiration, and I couldn't love her more.

None of this would have been possible without our families. Mom, Dad, Gloria, Krista, John, Melanie, Joe, Nolan, and Geena, your support through our toughest days is appreciated more than you will ever know. Whether you were with us physically or in spirit, you weathered many storms alongside us.

The love of family is one of the most important things we will ever have in our lives. I cherish ours.

Thank you to my friend and editor, HBW. Your insight and expertise are greatly appreciated.

Deer on a Tote Road

Main Character List

Nick Joseph - Main character, who was victimized
    Yve Joseph - Nick's wife and advocate
    Kenzie Joseph - Nick and Yve's young daughter
    Gloria - Nick's Mom and a retired nurse who lives in the mid-west/Kenzie calls her Nanny
    Nolan - Nick's Twin who lives in the mid-west
        Geena - Nolan's wife
        Eliza - Nolan's daughter
    Melanie – Nick's sister who lives in the mid-west
        Joe - Melanie's husband
        Jeremy – Melanie and Joe's son
        Nikki – Melanie and Joe's daughter, Mom to Jayden
    Mom and Dad – Yve's parents who live close to Yve and Nick/Kenzie calls them Mema and Poppy
    Krista - Yve's sister who lives next door to Yve and Nick
        John - Krista's Husband
        Gwen - Krista and John's young daughter

Brandon – Nick's Friend, ex-coworker, and hunting buddy
    Cary – Brandon's wife and Yve's best friend
    Elizabeth and Marissa – Brandon and Cary's children

Nick's Doctors and Nurses:
    Dr. Case - First Surgeon to treat Nick at Harris Hospital/Plastic Surgeon
    Dr. Bennett – Oral Maxillo-Facial Surgeon who treats Nick for years
    Myles, R.N. & Edie, R.N. – nurses who abuse Nick
    Rachel, R.N. – Nick's favorite nurse at Harris Hospital
    Sheila, R.N. – Nick's first home healthcare nurse
    Windy, R.N. – Nick's fantastic home healthcare nurse
    Dr. Dee – Nick's general practitioner at the time of the accident
    Jim, R.N. – nurse at the Emergency Room on the night of the accident
    Nancy, A.P.R.N. – Nick's diabetes nurse
    Dr. Carter – Plastic Surgeon/Dr. Case's senior partner who works with Dr. Bennett to repair Nick

Main Character List – continued

Dr. Jacobs – Harris Hospital Endocrinologist
Dr. Mallon – Orthopedic Surgeon who operated on Nick's shin

Friends Who Made the Journey Easier:
    Kyle – Nick's co-worker and close friend to all
    Dean – Nick's co-worker and close friend to all
        Tammy – Dean's wife and close friend to all
        Monica – Dean and Tammy's pre-teen daughter
        Collin – Dean and Tammy's young son
    Lisa – Nick's Deputy Warden who has a savvy with Investigations
    Erica – Yve's high school friend and Kenzie's school librarian

Surgical Consultants:
    Dr. Caron – plastic surgeon/second opinion
    Dr. Unid – oral surgeon/third opinion
    Dr. Sven – oral maxillo-facial surgeon/fourth opinion
    Dr. Felix – oral maxillo-facial surgeon/fifth opinion

Prologue

When Nicholas and Yve married in the summer of 2000, they both knew that they wanted a family. They also knew that there was an enormous possibility that that would never happen with their family infertility issues. Both were willing to do whatever it took to have that cherished family.

They tried artificial insemination multiple times. Adoption was considered every time that the test came back negative. Tears were shed as both wondered what they had done to deserve this sadness.

Their next step was Invitro Fertilization. Yve had high anxiety over the testing and total lack of modesty that goes with that experience. The night that Nicholas had to give her the final injection prior to egg retrieval, she was in tears worrying that their timing would be off, or something would go wrong...

But it didn't. In the Spring of 2003, their beautiful little girl, Kenzie, was born. The happiness they felt over this little bundle of joy was unimaginable. They lay awake at night watching that little chest rise and fall, wondering how they had gotten so lucky. They spent every available moment enjoying the wonderful journey of parenthood.

When their daughter was eighteen months old, they decided to try Invitro Fertilization for a second time using a frozen embryo from their first attempt. Sadly, a brother or sister for their daughter was not in the cards with that attempt.

They decided to start fresh one more time. One more round of shots, one more retrieval, and transfer of an embryo. One more round of Progesterone injections every day until that oh so scary pregnancy test.

Little did they know that their world would almost stop within 48 hours of that embryo transfer....

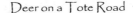

My Ponderings...

Did you ever want to take back a day in your life? You know, change the vital details that would alter the course of events in your life. I think of that frequently. What would have happened if I said "No, I don't want you to go hunting." If we hadn't argued about the snowy roads and that fact that he wanted me to be home, safe, but felt it was OK for him to drive twenty minutes from home to hunt.

If we hadn't just gone through Invitro again and he hadn't called in sick to work so I could have the prescribed forty-eight hours of bedrest. After all, we had a healthy nineteen-month-old. Were we pushing fate to ask for another child? If he had gone to work, it would have never happened. He would not have hunted that day. He would not have been standing in that spot, waiting for his friend to aim and shoot him.

The day would have been like any other…but life as we know it will never be the same. The chain of events which that one act set forth has changed our lives and those of the people around us forever.

Sunday, December 19, 2004

    Nicholas has been so supportive all weekend long. One more day of bedrest and hopefully our little embryo will be attached!

    Nick spent the day playing with our daughter, Kenzie. I love watching the interaction between those two. They were playing with her colorful wooden blocks on the floor, building towers for her to knock down. Both were wearing Santa hats and would stop frequently to gently knock heads for "hat kisses". Watching Kenzie giggle and the look on Nick's face every time they did it absolutely warmed my heart.

    He's such an awesome Dad. The thought that we may have just made her a little brother or sister has us so hopeful and excited!

    It was hard for me to just lay there, but it will all be worth it, even the "lovely" daily Progesterone injections, if we can have another child.

Monday, December 20, 2004, ~ morning

    Since I am laying here, waiting for my 48 hours of bedrest to end, I figured I would start my journal entry for today. My day will officially start at 11:30 am, when I can get up. In the meantime, Nick has gotten Kenzie dressed and fed. He surprised us this morning by running out to buy doughnuts for breakfast. Her little face is covered in chocolate. Those little rosy cheeks and bright eyes just make me so happy.

    Nick's buddy, Brandon, called a little while ago and asked him to go hunting. Nick is excited. It's a piece of property on which the landowner only permits law enforcement to hunt. The owner has mapped out the acreage, is very orderly in the organization of the hunting areas, and who is allowed to hunt where. The perfect spot according to Nick.

    I told Nick to go. Once I'm up, Kenzie and I might even go grocery shopping.

Monday, December 20, 2004, ~ 11:45am

    Nick left to meet Brandon. They're grabbing a pizza for lunch before hunting. He called me to tell me to stay home because the roads are covered in snow. I told him to come home too. It's not worth taking chances just to hunt. He told me he'd be fine, and we argued. I am so sick of this hunting garbage! He gets in a state of mind during hunting season where he feels he needs to go and make the most of the season when he has a day off. I realize that the seasons are relatively short, and he works a lot, but getting a deer is not worth risking your life on snowy roads.
    Kenzie and I will stay home safe and maybe even get some Christmas cookies baked. It's going to be a sweatpants kind of day.

Monday, December 20, 2004, ~ bedtime entry

    This afternoon, while Kenzie and I finished baking our batch of cookies, my dad came by to plow our driveway for us. While he was here, I heard a knock at the door. I thought it was Dad just coming in to hug us before he left. It was Dad, but there was also a state trooper standing by his side. Dad was crying uncontrollably. My heart sank. The officer told me that Nick had been shot. They didn't know if he was going to live. Dad said he would take Kenzie and I was to go with the officer. I hyperventilated while I rushed to throw on jeans and run to the cruiser.
    The officer was extremely nice to me. He explained as much as he knew, which was very little. I remember just staring at his cruiser radio and trying to focus. We headed North on the highway toward the hospital. I was scared to death when he suddenly did a U-Turn in the northbound lane to drive the wrong way down the highway for about fifty feet to get off the exit and head back south.
    Plans had changed. Nick was being flown to a larger hospital due to the extent of his injuries. The officer sympathetically told me that until we got there, we would not know if Nick was alive as they never share that information over the radio.
    We got lost for fifteen minutes enroute to the hospital. That drive was endless. The officer was wonderful in keeping me as calm as possible. When we got to the Emergency Room, the nurse there, who had no personality OR compassion told the officer, "You'll just have to wait! I'm busy!" To see the look on the officer's face was to know what a compassionate man he truly was.
    Ten minutes later, we found out that Nick was alive and in CT scan. We were escorted to a family waiting area in the Intensive Care Unit (I.C.U.). My parents and one of Nick's coworkers were already there. Kenzie was safe with my sister and brother-in-law.
    Slowly, I started to learn the events of the afternoon. Nick is a Corrections Officer and Brandon is a State Trooper. An Employee Assistance Person came to the hospital and started asking me if I wanted to see Brandon or not. I said, "Of course, he's the last person to see my husband whole." It was not until that moment that anyone

told me that it was Brandon who had shot Nick. I have no idea how I could have cried even harder, but I did.

When I saw him, I felt so bad for Brandon. He was a total mess. He was crying uncontrollably, sitting there with his wife, Cary, my best friend. It seems so crazy that she and I were just on the phone this afternoon. We were planning our mild-mannered New Year's Eve together since they are expecting their first child and we have Kenzie. How can this be happening?

I was pulled from the Family Waiting Room by the Emergency Room Surgeon to advise me of Nick's condition. There is immense damage to his jaw and neck area. They needed to debride the area and stop the bleeding. A cricothyrotomy had been placed at the first hospital to give Nick an airway before he was flown to this hospital. It is too soon to know what will happen, but they let me see Nick before they took him to surgery. The doctor told me that Nick was conscious and aware of where he was.

He looked like a stranger, except for those beautiful blue eyes that I love and trust. He was so swollen. He had parts of his jaw covered in bloodied gauze. I caught a glimpse of his tongue hanging out from a hole under his chin. It's amazing he has survived this. I don't think that I have ever prayed this hard.

They took Nick for surgery, and I was hugged by people I have never met before. The Warden from Nick's workplace, his coworkers, and friends who had heard kept appearing out of nowhere all night. The trooper who drove me to the hospital stayed by my side well after his shift had ended. I am overwhelmed with the abundance of compassion and caring around me.

Mom and Dad took me home tonight. It was after 1am so I guess it's tomorrow. Mom is staying with me tonight. Kenzie is having her first sleep over ever at my sister, Krista's. I am very thankful for my family. I called Nick's twin brother, Nolan, his sister, and mother. Nolan and my mother-in-law will be flying here tomorrow.

I know I need to sleep but my mind is racing. I am so afraid of the unknown right now. I am exhausted, but restless. I just pray that the phone doesn't ring with news that I dread.

Tuesday, December 21, 2004

    During the night last night, I suddenly remembered that little embryo trying to nestle inside me. Nick is supposed to be here to give me my daily Progesterone shot. I was panicked wondering what to do. I called our fertility doctor, and he was less than optimistic. He told me that trauma and stress are not a healthy environment for an embryo to implant. He called in a prescription for an alternative form of the Progesterone until someone else could do my injections. Nick is the only person I have who has been trained to do them.
    I also called my office to let them know what happened. Though I have only worked one day a week as a dental hygienist since Kenzie was born, I have patients in my schedule for the next six months. I have no idea when I will be able to work again. I spoke to my office manager, then to my boss. He was unbelievably supportive and told me to let him know if they could help in any way. I am not to worry about my job. It will be there when I am ready to return. When I hung up the phone, I cried at his sincere generosity and caring.
    I was at the hospital by 9am after picking up Kenzie for a kiss and leaving her with my mother and father. Nick responded to me more today by nodding when I spoke to him, but there is so much oozing from his bandages. He is on a ventilator and has IV lines coming out of both arms. I am scared to death. Machines are keeping my best friend alive, and I could not feel more helpless.
    Thankfully his surgeon gave me a purpose. I spent the better part of the day organizing a Directed Donor Blood Bank for Nick. By enlisting our families and coworkers to donate blood, we are ensured it will be there for him when he needs it. If he doesn't need it, it will be used for other patients. It has given me a bit of peace knowing I can do SOMETHING.
    Brandon is not being allowed to see Nick as visiting is limited to direct family only. He and Cary spent the entire day in the Family Waiting Area to be near Nick for updates. I am so torn between my need to be near my husband and knowing that I should step out to give Brandon updates on Nick's condition. I feel bad for Brandon as he's an emotional wreck. The news media has been camped outside their home since last night as well.

When the doctor let me know that Nick's tongue is still attached, I tried to lighten the mood by teasing Brandon that he's lucky he didn't mess up our kissing. I got a bit of a smirk with that at least.

My brother-in-law, John, was a big help by picking up Nick's Mom, Gloria, and his twin brother, Nolan, at the airport. He brought them directly to the hospital and it was a huge relief to see them.

Now we wait. The doctors are contemplating doing surgery tomorrow, but are unsure. The three of us came home for the night around 8:30 pm. I appreciate having them both here with me to talk and cry with. These two people love this man like I do. They understand how afraid I am because they are too.

Wednesday, December 22, 2004

If you ever told me that I would let my mother-in-law give me a shot in the ass, I would have told you that you're nuts. But here we are. Gloria is a retired registered nurse and quite capable with a needle. Maybe this embryo has a chance after all.

Gloria, Nolan, and I dropped Kenzie off at my mom and dad's and went to see Nick. He was awake! He wrote us notes! I am so confused though. His notes don't make any sense. He wrote, "I deserve it. Dad would kill me." He's also worried about Brandon and Kenzie. He wanted to know if it was time for my pregnancy test yet. I'm so happy I got to tell him that I love him. The argument we had over the snowy roads has weighed heavily on my mind. I told him that we're okay and that he'll be okay too.

Nolan and my sister, Krista, donated blood today. Nick's sister, Melanie, and her son, Jeremy, drove eleven hundred miles to be here today. I felt so bad for Melanie because Nick got so worked up when he saw her, the doctor would not allow her back in the room. It was so bizarre. Nick and Melanie have always been close.

Nick was taken down for surgery. I gave him a kiss for good luck as they took him from me.

I tried to talk to Brandon while Nick was in surgery. He will not tell me how it happened. He said his lawyer won't let him. It took me by surprise when he said he has a lawyer. I don't understand. It was an accident and I NEED to know what happened to my husband. Why does he need a lawyer if it was an accident? Does he think that there will be charges against him? Did the police union recommend a lawyer? Honestly, I just want to know what happened!

Nick's surgery went well. They found that he has two-thirds of his jawbone present, so they placed an external fixator to hold things in place. The bullet from the black powder rifle that Brandon was using went in on Nick's right side and exited on his left, ripping flesh and exploding bone as it moved through his jaw, leaving a powder residue.

Nick looks like he is wearing the mask of a football helmet except the prongs are protruding through his skin. They placed orthodontic bands on his upper teeth and remaining lower teeth and wired his mouth shut. The surgeon is really a cosmetic surgeon and he told me that Nick has enough tissue to cover the holes. That is great news!

When I got home tonight, my answering machine was full of well wishes and my refrigerator was filled with meals from friends. Melanie, Jeremy, Gloria, Nolan, and I visited, and they had a chance to spend some time with Kenzie. Given that they don't get to see her very often, I am trying to see the bright side of this whole mess and enjoying their interactions.

Thursday, December 23, 2004

    I felt so guilty leaving Kenzie with my mom. She's so clingy and wants her Daddy too. I needed to see Nick though and she would be terribly frightened if she saw him right now.

    Gloria, Melanie, Jeremy, Nolan, and I went to the hospital first thing this morning. We found Nick scared to death of a particular nurse, Ella. He was wild eyed, and I felt helpless not knowing what happened or how to make it better. Nolan was upset seeing Nick like that as well and decided he would spend the night at the hospital to support his twin.

    Another nurse, Myles, has been treating Nick oddly too. For the past two days, I have noticed that he keeps increasing the radio volume in Nick's room whenever I step out to speak to Brandon. It's so loud when I return that it bothers my ears. I can only imagine how much it bothers Nick with the head pain that he must have. I turn it down only to find it loud the next time I step out.

    Myles also seems to be very forgetful when it comes to Nick's pain meds. The push button which gives Nick some control over his medications is always just out of reach or behind his bed when I come back into his room. When I ask Myles about it, he always replies, "Did I forget that again?" and he laughs.

    In the meantime, I am also worried about Cary. Brandon is a mess and Cary is losing weight. Brandon won't confide in her either. Her obstetrician is worried and so am I. My friend has tried so hard, as we have, to have a child.

    Nick continues to ask me about our pregnancy test. I reassure him that the test isn't until December 29th.

Friday, December 24, 2004

    I was frightened awake by Jeremy banging suitcases down the stairs at 5:20 this morning. I swear he hit every stair on the way down. He and Melanie headed home ahead of a winter storm.
    I'm glad that Melanie had a chance to visit with Nick before heading back. His initial reaction to her presence still has me boggled. But he has been better since and for that I am happy.
    Gloria and I headed to the hospital early to relieve Nolan so he could nap in the Family Waiting Room. Nick had been taken into surgery to revise his cricothyrotomy into a tracheotomy. They also placed a J-G tube which is a type of feeding tube so he can be fed. I felt horrible that I wasn't there before he went for surgery, but I am so glad that Nolan was.
    Nick could be coming home in two to three weeks. While I am very happy to hear that, I am scared to death that Kenzie could pull on his fixator.
    I sat by Nick's side for ten hours except for two, one half hour breaks to eat and console Brandon in the family waiting room. He still won't talk to me and though I understand the whole legal aspect of this, I truly feel he owes me an explanation of what happened. He almost killed my husband!
    Nick was so uncomfortable today. He was very antsy this afternoon and keeps having nightmares. I feel so helpless.
    To be honest, I am heartbroken that I spent Christmas Eve away from Kenzie. She went with my parents to my aunt's house and was completely fine, but I wasn't. They called me from my aunt's so everyone could talk, especially Kenzie. I am so torn between being with my husband and being with my child. It's excruciating.
    Gloria, Nolan, and I came home tonight to spend Christmas morning with Kenzie. We have asked Santa to hold off coming until Nick is home, but I still want a bit of special time with my girl.
    Nolan and I sat and chatted for quite a while tonight. He is a police officer back home, as well as a hunter. He had insight as to what might have happened, though neither of us will have a clue until Nick can at least tell us what he remembers. Just from what Nolan said tonight, something is off. Nick is a very cautious hunter.

Saturday, December 25, 2004

Nolan, Gloria, and I tried to make this morning special for Kenzie. We only let her open three of the maroon, wrapped boxes tied neatly with jute bows that included clothes and one toy. I tried so hard not to cry as she danced around the kitchen singing to her new refrigerator magnet toy while my only thought was, Nick is missing this.

Nolan, Gloria, and I dropped Kenzie off at my parent's house on the way to the hospital. The three of them will join Krista's family for Christmas dinner.

When I got to the hospital, I was in no way prepared for what was waiting for me. Nick was frantic. He was writing irrational notes to me. "They've been torturing me all day." "They're injecting me." "They'll hurt you too." It's so scary to see him like that. I kept reassuring him, but he just continued to look at me with wild eyes that were so fearful it was palpable.

As I sat there trying to comfort him, I started to take in his surroundings. His left arm was very swollen, and the top of his head had a bloodied area that previously did not exist. He's actually bald in that spot like road rash. I KNOW that didn't exist before. I have been using cool cloths to wipe him down to make him more comfortable for days. I would have noticed that.

I questioned Nick's trauma surgeon, asking if it could be post-traumatic stress, and he had no explanations. He just told me that the pain medications may have Nick hallucinating. Now I am even more worried. So is Nolan. He cancelled his flight home.

Sunday, December 26, 2004

  Nick came off the ventilator today!! He was moved out of Intensive Care and into the Step-Down Unit. He is starting to look like himself and seems less frightened now that he is away from the Intensive Care nurses.

  He asked if it was time to take our pregnancy test yet and I told him "Not yet." Gloria teased him about giving me my Progesterone shots and her enjoyment in doing so. He smirked and it was nice to see.

  Nolan is spending the night at the hospital and will continue to do that until his twin feels comfortable. I thank God for Nolan. I can't be two places at once and Kenzie needs to see at least one of her parents.

  I know that my sister-in-law, Geena, is upset that Nolan made the decision to stay. She is seven months pregnant with their first child and wants Nolan home with her. While I completely understand, I feel bad for Nolan when I can tell that she will not speak to him on the phone, but just gives him the silent treatment. He is scared for his brother and could really use her support right now.

  Tomorrow, they plan to move Nick to a regular room. I am praying that Nick can get past his fear as the hospital view changes. His doctor ordered a psychological evaluation to investigate his fearfulness further.

Tuesday, December 28, 2004

I spent the day with Nick. The psychiatrist came to evaluate him. After she was done, she talked to me privately. She told me that Nick wrote, "Well it wasn't suicide." She asked if I knew what that meant. I had no idea what he was getting at, but then again, we had never discussed the accident. I had been way too afraid to upset him even more.

I decided it was time to talk. I mentioned to Nick the note that he had written to the psychiatrist and asked what it meant. Slowly, the story unfolded, and I realized that Nick didn't know what had happened. He was always so cautious when hunting. His father had always demanded that. He wrote that the only thing he could think of was maybe his trigger had been tripped by a branch.

The realization of the reason my poor husband was having nightmares hit me like a storm. He thought he shot himself!

Nolan brought Nick into the hospital bathroom and had him look in the mirror. He asked him how he could have shot himself. The wound would have been south to north.

As we explained that Brandon had thought he was a deer and shot him, we could see the weight being lifted off of him. His whole demeanor changed.

I cannot begin to explain the look of relief on his face. He had been completely distraught with himself for putting his family through all of this. He wrote down everything that he remembered from that afternoon, and I slowly started filling him in on the little bit that Brandon had shared. Nolan asked him questions that I would have never thought to ask about where he was in relation to Brandon, what Brandon was using for a gun, etc. Today was definitely a turning point for Nick and a huge relief for Nolan, Gloria, and me.

Wednesday, December 29th, 2004

I am preparing for Nick to come home. I met a very kind woman from Human Resources at the jail where Nick works and she has been wonderful.

At first, the hospital was pressuring me to put Nick in a convalescent home. They felt it would be unsafe for him to come home with a tracheotomy and the level of care he needs while I have a nineteen-month-old to care for as well.

Gloria came to our rescue by offering to stay with us as long as she's needed. What an absolute Godsend! I know that she is Nick's mom, and she feels she needs to be here, but I think that it's a huge sacrifice for her to leave her home for an extended period, not knowing when she will return.

Today was my pregnancy test. Nick has been asking, "Is it the 29th yet?", every day. I can't believe he remembers with everything he is going through.

When I went to have blood drawn this morning, they had trouble finding my vein. That has never happened before. They said it could be the stress or the fact that I've lost ten pounds in the last nine days. The result came back by noon. It was negative. It's odd, but I am unaffected by the negative test. I have too many bigger concerns. I was so sick when I was pregnant for Kenzie. God knows what he's doing, Nick needs me now and so does Kenzie.

I spent most of the afternoon and evening learning how to do Nick's care once he gets home. My parents brought Kenzie to see him for the first time. She was apprehensive when she saw his tracheostomy and external fixator. I gave her some lotion to rub on his feet and she started to help "take care of Daddy". It was very sweet.

Once Kenzie left, Nick asked to see Brandon and Cary. They have been sitting in the Family Waiting Room religiously every day. The visit was very emotional for all of us. Nick wrote notes on his whiteboard, and I could see he was trying to make Brandon feel better. He's a good man.

Nolan has been sleeping at the hospital every night. He flew home today and though I know he belongs with my pregnant sister-in-law; he has been such a great shoulder to cry on and we are all going to miss him. Geena is due for their first child in March, and she needs him there.

	Nick's friend, Kyle, has offered to stay with him at night when he isn't working. Nick's fear to be alone at this hospital is still very real and we all agreed that he will heal better without that extra stress.

Thursday, December 30, 2004

I took down the Christmas decorations this morning. Dad and Brandon came over to rearrange the furniture in our living room to make room for the hospital bed that will be delivered.

Dad and I went to see Nick around 10 am. Kyle had left early this morning to get some things done before coming back tonight. I don't think he'll ever realize how much his staying means to us.

Nick was having a very tough day. His tracheostomy went bad and had to be replaced. It took his trauma surgeon four tries to find one that fit. Poor Nick stopped breathing for seconds every time they tried a new one. It was so scary to watch, and Nick was exhausted when the surgeon was finished. Nick also became very paranoid again.

Kyle returned tonight. We chatted about the day and his overnight stay with Nick last night. Kyle told me about Nick's need to use the commode during the night and how he didn't want Nick to get out of bed without nurse help due to the tubes, hoses, and cords. Kyle grabbed the first nurse he saw for the job. Both he and Nick agreed that she was wonderful. She got Nick to the commode and even wiped his bottom with warm washcloths when he was done.

As Kyle was relating the story, a uniformed woman walked into Nick's bathroom and then left. Nick pointed toward the door and Kyle said, "That's the nurse who helped." I just about fell out of my chair laughing. Neither of them had a clue what I was laughing about, until I told them that she wasn't a nurse but in fact a member of the maintenance staff. Nick cracked us up further by writing,
"No wonder she was so good at cleaning up!" All I can say is God bless that very kindhearted soul. Not only did she show immense compassion and caring for my husband, which wasn't even her job, but she also gave me the first good laugh since the accident. That laughter, for all of us, was very needed.

Friday, December 31, 2004, ~ New Year's Eve

My parents and Kenzie joined Gloria and I for our daily visit with Nick today. He and Kenzie played a bit and she rubbed his feet with lotion again. After a while, my parents took Kenzie home with them.

I learned how to suction Nick's tracheostomy today. To say it scares me to death is an understatement. Knowing he will rely on me to clear his airway so he can breathe once he comes home is daunting. The nurses taught me to clean the pins that protrude from the skin on his jaw, all six of them, and how to dress his wounds.

Brandon came to the hospital later this afternoon and we played Scrabble with Nick and Gloria. Gloria is a formidable Scrabble opponent and it made me laugh inside to see the glimmer in Nick's eyes when he bested her.

Tonight, I rubbed Nick's back before I left. I couldn't help crying. I miss him so much. Yes, I see him daily, but we have such limited physical contact. I'm afraid to even kiss the top of his head; I know he hurts.

The hospital staff brought in a cot for Gloria to sleep on tonight. Kyle had to work, and I needed to be home for Kenzie. Gloria insisted on staying so Brandon drove me home.

The ride home was an awkward one. Brandon barely said two words and I couldn't bare the silence, so I chatted and tried to focus the conversation on their unborn baby and Cary.

When I got home, there was a package from Melanie with all the clothes that Gloria had requested inside. I am so thankful for Melanie's help to make this easier for Gloria and me.

I knew I wouldn't be able to sleep, so I cleaned out the shelves of the entertainment center in our living room to make room for medical supplies.

Saturday, January 1, 2005

Nick made short trips around the halls of the hospital with me today. I learned to dispense his medications through his feeding tube. I feel like I'm back in college with the amount of note taking that I'm doing. So much depends on how well I take care of him.

Today was the first time that Nick shared what he now remembered about the accident. He wrote that he and Brandon had hunted together until fifteen minutes before it happened. They parted ways and agreed to meet on a logging tote road. Nick got there first and was standing with the butt of his gun on his boot, just looking around.

Suddenly, his upper torso was whipped around by the impact of the lead shot that ripped through his lower jaw. He was knocked on his back and only heard the rapport of the gun after he felt the impact. He struggled to his knees to get the blood out of his airway.

Brandon thought he had shot a deer and radioed Nick on the walkie talkie to tell him. Nick could only gurgle in reply. Realizing what he had done, Brandon ran to him. He told Nick to stay put and he would get help.

Since Nick had driven them there, he threw his truck keys to Brandon, and Brandon ran off into the woods toward the truck. Nick wasn't just going to sit there so he got up, tucked his chin which was bleeding profusely, into his chest, and started walking down the tote road. He knew it led to a paved road and he had to get help for himself. He wrote to me that in his mind, he could hear his deceased father tell him, "Get a move on Boy!"

Nick walked half a mile to the paved road and flagged down a snowplow. Behind that snowplow was an off-duty state trooper. It was the very same trooper who had helped us install Kenzie's toddler car seat not eight months earlier.

The trooper treated Nick like a son, holding him upright until the ambulance came. At first, he tried to get Nick to lay down, but Nick struggled to show him that he couldn't breathe if he laid down.

The officer also flagged down a moving van and grabbed a blanket to cover Nick in the hope of keeping him from going into shock. The poor moving van driver was reluctant to stop at first. Nick told me that he was a black man, and when he saw a man bleeding, he was afraid to be blamed. How sad is the world that we live in?

Thank God Nick walked out and didn't wait. Brandon, in his panic and despair, got lost in the woods. Nick was already loaded in the ambulance before the landowner found Brandon.

This story brought me to tears. In my head, I could only hear my husband gurgling.

These long days and hour-long rides to and from the hospital, coupled with the sleepless nights and stress, have us exhausted. Gloria and I got home around 9 pm tonight. I am wiped out. I am so happy that Mom and Dad got Kenzie bathed and in bed before I got home.

Sunday, January 2, 2005

Another day of preparations for Nick's return home. Our favorite nurse, Rachel, helped me to make lists of supplies. She also helped me make a chart for the order in which his care needs to be done. I will be hanging all this information on clipboards in the living room for easy reference.

Dad came with Gloria and I today. He has a tough time seeing Nick like this. I can see that he wants to cry, and it breaks my heart.

Brandon and Cary visited today. The look of exhaustion on Cary's face has me very worried about my friend and her pregnancy. She always hugs me and smiles, but I know from our limited conversations alone, she is going through this pregnancy and stress with the help of her parents and not Brandon.

Gloria is spending the night at the hospital tonight. Dad drove me home, where Mom and Kenzie were waiting for us. While I was gone, one of Nick's coworkers had stopped by. They had taken up a collection at work and he presented my mom with over two thousand dollars to help us pay medical bills. I started to cry. I am completely overwhelmed with their generosity. I know Nick will be too when I tell him tomorrow. So many people have reached out to comfort or help in one form or another. I just hope they all know how much it means to us.

Monday, January 3, 2005

When I got to the hospital today, it was obvious that nurse Rachel was the only organized person on the floor. The doctors had told Nick he could go home but the Pulmonary doctor had issues with him leaving. It was like one hand didn't know what the other hand was doing.

Nick's feeding tube pump came to his room, and I had lessons on how to use it. I am so tense about Nick coming home. I just hope that I can keep everything straight.

Brandon came to visit and then helped me to carry supplies to my car. Nick's boss, the warden, visited along with one of his captains. Nick told them that he's lucky to have me. I just hope I can live up to his praise.

Tuesday, January 4, 2005

My Dad and I stopped at A-1 medical supply store to pick up a suction for Nick's tracheostomy. His trauma surgeon had called in the prescription yesterday, but they wouldn't deliver in time, so we had to pick it up.

We went to the hospital and waited for Nick to be released. It took four hours for the paperwork to be completed. Poor Nick was exhausted just waiting around.

Dad and I got Nick home safely and someone from A-1 delivered a humidifier for Nick's tracheostomy. I changed Nick's dressings and did his feeding tube care.

He ended up having a breathing issue with his trach once he was situated in our living room in the hospital bed. I hurried to suction to remove the mucous while his feet went up in the air with frustration and fear. I got it! Then I ran to the bathroom to throw up. I was so scared that I wouldn't clear his airway, I actually threw up.

The closest ambulance is twelve minutes away. If I can't clear his airway, he will die before they get here. I am scared to death and that anxiety hit my stomach like a tsunami.

Wednesday, January 5, 2005, ~ Nick's first full day at home

I got up at 4 am to suction Nick's trach. I am giving him Tussin every four hours to keep his secretions loose. I filled his feeding tube pump with another can of formula and went back to bed.

My bed is now a twin mattress and box spring on the living room floor, located about three feet from Nick's hospital bed. I was so restless all night last night. I lay there worrying about him and listening to his breathing. I'm petrified that his breathing will stop, especially when help is about twelve minutes away.

I was showered and ready when our visiting nurse, Sheila, arrived at 8:30 this morning. She did Nick's wound care, pin care, trach care and feeding tube care. She also ordered supplies for us. The hospital never gave us an inner canula for Nick's trach. An inner canula fits inside the trach and can be removed to be cleaned and replaced to avoid Nick's airway from being blocked. How could the hospital send him home without one? Thank God for Sheila! She ordered two inner cannulas for us and I'm hoping that this will reduce my stress level.

Sheila was very informative and motherly. When she left at noon, I was finally able to eat breakfast…or lunch. Thankfully mom kept Kenzie for two hours this morning which allowed Gloria and I to get a full grasp on the information that Sheila gave us.

I was so busy with Nick today I could barely breathe. Sheila came back at 4pm and Brandon came over too. It's so awkward when Brandon's around. He just sits in silence. Poor Nick practically writes a book on his whiteboard for his part of their conversation and Brandon just gives him one-word answers. It exhausts Nick but he feels so bad for Brandon that he keeps trying to draw him out to talk.

Gloria made dinner for herself, Kenzie, and me. My parents came over and my mom gave Kenzie a bath while dad ran to the pharmacy for Nick's prescriptions. My sister, John, and our niece, Gwen came over with a floor style work lamp and a pushcart with shelves to put Nick's trach humidifier, medications, suction, and supplies on. They were absolute lifesavers! These items made everything more orderly for me.

Finally, at 10pm, I gave Nick his last medications until 2 am. Now to get some sleep…

Thursday, January 6, 2005

    We had a rough night last night. Nick's feeding tube pump alarm kept going off. I was up at 12 am, 1:30 am, 2 am, 4 am, and 6 am. I finally got up and got dressed at 7:15 am. I did Nick's trach and feeding tube care by myself then I actually got some snuggle time in with Kenzie. That was the best 20 minutes I have had in quite a while!
    In between doing laundry and cleaning the house, two visiting nurses came. They watched me do Nick's pin care and wound care. His pin care consists of using a peroxide mixture to clean around each of the six external fixator pins while also pressing his tissue away from the pins a bit so that the tissue doesn't grow around them.
    His wound care consists of removing twelve inches of gauze from the whole under his chin, cleaning the area with sterile saline, then packing the area again with twelve more inches of sterile gauze soaked in sterile saline. The reasoning behind this is to remove dead tissue from inside the hole with the dried-out gauze and replace it with clean.
    It's my responsibility to take care of Nick, and the visiting nurses' responsibility to be sure that I'm doing it right. I must do this care three times a day, and most of the time they won't be here. This care is in conjunction with cleaning his trach, filling his feeding tube pump, dispensing his medications via his feeding tube, filling his trach humidifier, and cleaning all the medical equipment.
    Mom sent beef stew for supper tonight. Having them and Gloria around constantly can be tough sometimes. After all, most married couples don't basically live with their parents. I get irritated from time to time, but I honestly couldn't ask for better support. They have been wonderful.

Friday, January 7, 2005

    Gloria and I set up our equipment cleaning regiment today. My Obsessive-Compulsive Disorder is finally coming in handy. Keeping this all straight is quite an undertaking. Having Gloria here to help is a huge plus.
    We had yet another visiting nurse today. She was an hour late and a bull in a China shop. She insisted on doing Nick's care to give me a break. Worst of all, she was sweating so badly under the shop light, when she did some of Nick's care, I actually saw sweat droplets land on his open wound under his chin. She made me an absolute wreck! After having the importance of keeping whatever touches that hole sterile drilled into my brain, it was horrifying.
    My neighbor, Eloise, took Gloria grocery shopping today and my parents brought takeout food for supper. The evening went well until Nick's trach occluded again tonight. It seemed like a lifetime before I got his airway cleared. Once again, I threw up immediately after I knew he was ok.

Saturday, January 8, 2005

Santa Claus came today!

Since Nick felt well enough to sit and watch Kenzie open her gifts today, I laid everything out in the sunroom while she napped this afternoon. It was so strange to see a filled Christmas stocking and brightly colored packages on the floor in January.

I moved Nick's trach humidifier into the sunroom and got him situated in a recliner. My parents and Gloria joined us and I'm so happy we waited to celebrate this as a family.

It was exhausting for Nick to sit up for two hours, but I could see the joy in his eyes while he watched Kenzie unwrap her gifts. Our child is very animated and was excited over her gifts.

Tomorrow, Krista, John, and Gwen will come over to exchange gifts with us too.

Today is the first day since the accident that we didn't see or hear from Brandon at all. That was perfect timing as we really needed the family time.

Wednesday, January 12, 2005

The last three days have been crazy busy. On Monday, I managed to break the only pair of prescription eyeglasses that I own. Thank God Cary works at my optometrist's office! She came to my rescue by picking them up, picking out a new frame for me, having the old lenses put in, and returning them to me at night. Thank God for contact lenses during the day and a best friend who knows me well enough to pick out a perfect pair of frames for me!

I also had my own doctor appointment, and it was the first time I left the house since Nick came home. I was a nervous wreck leaving him, even though he was with Gloria.

Tuesday included a trip to the hospital with Nick, Gloria, and my dad for follow up appointments with the plastic surgeon and trauma surgeon. Both were pleased with Nick's progress.

Every day is otherwise pretty much the same. Twelve to fourteen hours of Nick's care, laundry, housework, and a little time with Kenzie. I miss her even though we are in the same house.

Today, among the regularly scheduled events of the day, we had a visit from a State Police Detective and an Officer from the Department of Environmental Protection. They came to question Nick about the accident as they were the ones heading the investigation. They asked Nick to identify which hunting gear was his in the pictures that they provided. They had aerial photos of the scene of the accident and wanted him to point out where he was standing and where Brandon was. The questions they asked were repetitive as well as intimidating.

Poor Nick started to hyperventilate on his trach when he was writing information on his white board, and they didn't seem to understand what he was saying. A couple of times, I intervened to interpret what I thought he was saying, and he hurriedly nodded yes and pointed at me.

Nick told me later that he felt they were trying to get him to say something against Brandon. At the time, all I saw was Nick getting extremely worked up and struggling to breathe. It was a nightmare.

I know that they need to sort everything out, but Nick is still so weak. I hope they don't need to speak with him again for a while. Nick verified that he has no intention of pressing charges. It was an accident.

Thursday, January 13, 2005

One of Nick's coworkers came by with yet another donation from the Department of Corrections. Those people are simply amazing, and we are so humbled by their generosity.

Nick stunned me today by writing a long narrative about the mistreatment he received while in the hospital, in the Intensive Care Unit, at the hands of the nurses. While I had questioned his anxiety while he was there, the detail in his account today has me convinced that there was abuse on Christmas Day.

Nick has been so affected by these nurses. While he has written small bits and pieces every day, today he wrote everything on paper. His anger is palpable. The open sore on the top of his head is a testament to what happened. I wonder if he'll ever get hair back in that spot.

Honestly, I think he is more upset about the abuse than the accident. As he wrote, the nurses hurt him while he was unable to protect himself. They did small things during his entire stay in I.C.U. but on Christmas morning he endured literal torture for hours.

Before it started, Nurse Myles asked Nick if he was having any visitors that morning. Nick told him, "No." The nurses then took him to another floor with an observation window where they could watch him. They had him in restraints on a table, but only on his left side. They dropped the table and Nick hung by his arm and leg. They left him there for a long period of time. His IVs came out and that was why his arm was bruised and swollen. When they returned, they loosened the restraints, and he was dropped on his head. That is when the abrasion to his head happened.

When Nick was returned to his room, Nurse Myle's girlfriend, Nurse Edie told Nick, "Merry Christmas. That was my idea." That cold hearted witch.

After reading the details of his ordeal, my heart is broken for him. To think I thought he was experiencing PTSD and initially dismissed the abuse as his mind playing games, also breaks my heart.

Saturday, January 15, 2005

Nick's feeding tube got blocked by his medications this morning. I put a call out to our visiting nurse, and I was amazed to learn that 7Up helps to unblock it. Of course, she returned my call only after I became a nervous wreck that it's the weekend and I needed to feed him and give him his medications. My anxiety might just be the death of me.

Nick's wound is getting deeper and sorer. I am placing thirteen inches of gauze in it now. I'm worried that it will never heal.

We had a visit from Brandon and Cary today. Brandon took down the icicle lights on the front of the house for me. He barely talks. I wish he would tell us what happened. I feel so bad for Cary. This is supposed to be such a happy time in their lives, expecting their first child. It is anything but happy.

Monday, January 17, 2005

The visiting nurses still come three times a week. For the most part, it feels like a social occasion now. I do all of Nick's care while they chat with us. They take my list of needed supplies and have it sent to us too.

Nick's trach humidifier quit on us, so A-1 delivered a new one. Thankfully they delivered the same day that it stopped working. That humidifier helps keep his secretions thinner and breathing easier.

When I went to give Kenzie a bath tonight, I found that we had no hot water. I thought, what else?!? Thankfully, we discovered that Gloria had switched off the emergency switch for the boiler instead of the basement lights. The switch is directly over the light switch so I can see where it might happen if you're not used to it.

There was an easy fix for a problem for a change and I hate to admit it, but I had fun teasing Gloria for a bit too.

Tuesday, January 18, 2005

Good gravy it's a lot of work to get Nick to the doctor's office! We need someone to drive so that I can sit in the back seat with Nick in case I need to suction his trach. That means we always have his suction machine, and often his trach humidifier, with us.

Today we went to see his plastic surgeon, Dr. Case. He has been the main surgeon in charge since that horrible night in the Emergency Room. Dr. Case feels that Nick is doing well, but prefers that we reschedule to see the Oral Maxillofacial Residents. He wants them to review everything and help him determine when to unwire Nick's jaw. He just doesn't feel that it's stable enough yet. We will see him in one week.

The running back and forth is exhausting. It's an hour in each direction plus the stress of the ride on Nick.

My responsibilities seem endless. I run from early morning until late at night. Not only do I care for Nick, but I still have Kenzie to care for as well as three dogs to feed. It's been a snowy month and I feel like I shovel several times a week not to mention cooking, cleaning, and bringing in wood. But, as overwhelmed as I feel, what the heck would I do if I didn't get the help I do?

Gloria helps with Kenzie, meals, and some cleaning too. Mom and Dad still come by frequently to help too. Nick refuses to let his mom do any of his care. Though she is a retired registered nurse, her hands are very arthritic, and she tends to be a bit rough when doing his care. She doesn't mean to, but her hands simply won't let her do anything else.

Tuesday, January 25, 2005

Kenzie has been waking up, crying, at 12:30 am every night for the last two weeks. The poor kid is disoriented by all of this, but she is still happy go lucky during the day. She even started drinking from a "big girl" cup instead of her sippy cup sometimes!

Gloria and I made a group effort today to cut Nick's hair. We were all afraid to get hair in his trach so while I trimmed, she stood there with the central vacuum and sucked everything up like a dental assistant. Crazy as it was, it worked, and Nick feels much better. Ingenuity pays off! Showers are scary as heck too. I am afraid to drown him through his trach. Thank God we have a handheld shower!

Cleaning messes seems to be par for the course today. As I was drawing up a syringe of Nick's medications to put in his feeding tube, the vacuum suction in the tube had the meds shoot out like a rocket. They hit my ceiling and dripped down my kitchen cabinets. I couldn't help but cry.

I am trying to get a bit more sleep by altering the timing of Nick's medications. I have been dispensing them at 4am, 10am, 4pm, and 10pm. The new schedule is 6am, 12pm, 6pm, and 11pm. Hopefully, with more sleep, my anxiety will calm down.

Of course, Gloria has been teasing me because of my new catch phrase, "It's a non-issue." I don't know where I came up with it, but man, do I say it a LOT!

Monday, January 31, 2005

  Due to snowy roads, Nick, my dad, and I left at 8am for a 10am appointment with the Maxillofacial Surgeon, Dr. Bennett, up at Harris Hospital.
  We were there for forty minutes before the assistant came to tell us that the doctor wouldn't be coming in until 1pm. They put us in a recovery room, and I set up Nick's trach humidifier. Dad and I ate potato chips from the vending machine for lunch. Thankfully, I always carry a can of Nick's food and a syringe with me.
  When Dr. Bennett finally came, he decided to unwire Nick's jaw. I am heartbroken. His lower front teeth are obviously displaced, and his jaw is leaning to his left.
  This husband of mine used to have tiny, but perfect, teeth. As a dental hygienist, seeing what is in there now is heart wrenching. I know too much, yet not enough when it comes to Nick's current condition. Later, when I was alone, I cried for what used to be.

Tuesday, February 1, 2005

We went to the Dr. Case, the plastic surgeon today. He said that Nick is looking good and that there should be no reason to take tissue from a donor area to cover the hole in his chin. A hole that is still leaking saliva constantly.

He said that Nick should be out of the external fixator in two to three weeks, but he may need a small tissue graft under his tongue to close the hole. That seems unbelievable since the hole is still pretty big. I want to believe him, I need to.

The next step is to downsize Nick's trach. Neither of us can wait for the day that he can breathe without it!

For now, I am to work on cleaning the debris from Nick's tongue. After being wired shut for weeks, there is still blood debris covering it. I can only imagine how it tastes to Nick.

I feel like an idiot, but I broke down tonight. It seems like forever since I have had the time to give my own child a bath. Mom and Gloria have been awesome about stepping in to do anything I can't, but I MISS the special time with my girl.

This accident has had me torn in so many ways. Nick needs me, and I need to be with him. On the other hand, until the accident, the three of us had been together for her baths and now neither Nick nor I are taking part.

Wednesday, February 2, 2005

It feels like my car should have autopilot for the hour drive to and from the hospital. Today we went to the Trauma Clinic to have Nick's trach downsized to a metal one. Nick was able to cover the trach and say, "I love you." Hearing him speak meant more than I can ever say.

When we got home, he said, "Hi Kenzie". Though his voice sounds different, it is so great to hear him speak! Hopefully, the trach will come out next week.

Gloria and I had a difference of opinion today too. I've been so "by the book" when it comes to Nick's care. I follow the doctor's orders to the hilt. Gloria, on the other hand, has a nursing background that I don't. Sometimes it's hard to know what's right. The one thing that I can say is that we are pretty good at discussing things diplomatically.

I've also become very fond of our 9pm snack time once Kenzie and Nick are in bed. Gloria and I will have a snack, sometimes less than nutritious, and laugh, or cry, about the day. Our favorite snack around Christmas time was some of my mom's chocolate fudge and a glass of milk. We just sit at the bar in the kitchen and review the day together. As much as we can drive each other a bit crazy from time to time, it's a blessing to have someone here to discuss everything.

Sunday, February 6, 2005

Brandon came over to play Pitch with Nick today. He stayed to watch the first half of the Patriots vs. Eagles Superbowl XXIX. His visits are sparser now, maybe once a week or every other week. He sits on the recliner, near Nick's bed, with his head down. He occasionally will give Nick a side glance, or nod in answer to Nick's questions. He very rarely starts a conversation.

Honestly, it's better for all of us that he doesn't come as often now. His sadness and silence are very hard. The unknown has us nervous, but I can only imagine how he feels when he sees Nick. I wish he would seek out help. Cary needs him.

Tuesday, February 8, 2005

    One of Nick's coworkers and his Warden came to visit today. The Warden has been so supportive and helpful. It was heartwarming to see him get down on our floor to play with Kenzie. Kenzie enjoyed it too! Nick works with some truly awesome people!

    Something is going on with my own health, but I'm not sure what. I've been very nauseous and dizzy, on and off, for the past week. When I get up off the twin bed, I get so dizzy, I need to just sit there for a minute or two. My chest feels heavy and it's hard to breathe sometimes too. This has me very nervous. I can't afford to be sick when Nick relies on me so much, not to mention Kenzie!

Wednesday, February 9, 2005

    I'm worried. There was a lot of oozing from the hole in Nick's chin last night. It was a reddish-yellow color and slightly viscous. The hole is still about three-quarters of an inch round with red, rough tissue at its edges. I will feel better once we see Dr. Case. He has felt like a lifeline for all of us in this mess.
    We went to the trauma surgeon this morning. Nick's trach was removed! He still needs to wait for the hole to heal, but what an absolute relief! He spent the last week preparing for this. He had to cover the hole for a longer period of time every day to practice breathing without it. We both feel so much safer without that trach! No more suctioning then running to vomit!!
    A visit to the speech and swallow therapist was also on today's schedule. Unfortunately, there's not much that she can do to help him yet as he's not allowed any liquids orally. The hole in his chin needs to be healed before that can happen, and with the oozing that is happening, I am having a very hard time staying optimistic.
    Gloria continues to tease me about my mantra, "It's a non-issue." Every set back we have, has been met by those words. I cannot focus on the problems; I will lose my mind. I need to stay as positive as possible.

Thursday, February 10, 2005

    We went to see Dr. Case today. He feels that Nick is doing well. He may try to remove the external fixator and place a reconstructive titanium plate in one to two weeks.

    I asked him about using the directed donor blood. He stated that there should be no need for a blood transfusion, but he prefers not to use directed donor blood anyway. He feels that they don't test it as diligently as anonymous donor blood.

    Why weren't we told this before? I was told that whatever wasn't used for Nick could be used by others. Brandon and Cary gave us the two hundred and fifty dollars to set up the directed donor program for Nick. We also had several people donate to it. Now it will never be used. What a horrendous waste!

    Dr. Case agreed that I can use different bandages for Nick's chin. He's still leaking saliva, but the current bandage restricts movement. I have fashioned "hammocks" to sit under his chin and hook on his external fixator to hold gauze to keep him from dripping everywhere. I brought one with us for the doctor's approval. We tried it and Nick is happy with it.

    I ended the day by giving Kenzie a bath. Not a week ago I was crying because I didn't have the time to bathe her. My mom and Gloria were always doing it. This week, I've bathed her twice myself and she graced me by peeing in the tub both times. Maybe that's God's funny way of saying, "You cried for not being able to do it, now you can do it twice in an hour." Either way, I'm glad I'm doing it. Kenzie is the joy of my life. Without knowing it, she gets me through the day with her cute comments and hugs.

Friday, February 11, 2005

Windy, our primary visiting nurse, came today. She's been with us twice a week for a while now. The last visiting nurse got fired. Honestly, we weren't fond of her anyway. She was always late or didn't come period. Windy let us know that she had taken off with her laptop and patient information and the hospital was trying to track her down. One more thing to worry about, identity theft.

Windy, on the other hand, is a super nurse. She's extremely supportive and informative. She also loves Kenzie. Today, Windy took my blood pressure. Thankfully, it's fine. She's not sure why I'm so dizzy and nauseous, but she recommended that I try an antihistamine. She also told me a parable that I'm sure I'll never forget. It went something like this:

A caregiver has a basket of apples. Each time she helps her loved ones, she gives them an apple. If she doesn't take the time for herself, to replenish her basket, she'll run out of apples to give.

Sunday, February 13, 2005

  We resumed our family dinners at my parents' house tonight. It is a tradition in my family to have dinner with Krista, John, and Gwen at my parents' every Sunday. It has been almost two months, but it felt so wonderful to do something normal again. It was nice to have Gloria be part of our tradition. Krista and John even remarked how glad they were that we could all be together again. That meant a lot to me.
  I am looking forward to tomorrow too. Gloria will watch Kenzie while I go to work for an office meeting. It will be nice to see everyone! Nick's friend is picking him up to take one of our dogs for his annual vet appointment. It will be the first time that Nick leaves the house with anyone but me. Though I am a bit nervous about that, the fact that the trach is gone makes it one million times easier.

Thursday February 17, 2005

Nick will have surgery tomorrow! We are both scared and excited. I spent the morning arranging for the Trauma Surgeon to check on him while he's at Harris Hospital and letting nurse Rachel know he's coming. I also spoke to a nurse in admitting too.

Nick and I took a walk with Kenzie and played with her. My parents picked her up at 7:30pm. She's so excited to be sleeping over there. I, on the other hand, just want to cry. I've never been away from her at night except for the necessary times since the accident. My little shining light is very missed tonight.

Friday, February 18, 2005

Dad came to pick us up at 4:45am. Nick, Dad, Gloria, and I went to the hospital where Nick was admitted and brought to a changing area then Pre-Op. I was allowed in Pre-Op with him where I had the "pleasure" (feel the sarcasm) of watching them push a rubber hose up his nose and into his throat to intubate him. They can't intubate through his mouth because they are operating on his mouth and the tube would be in the way. Dr. Case had been called for another surgery, so he was an hour and a half late for Nick.

I sat in the Family Waiting Room with Dad and Gloria. After the surgery, Dr. Case came to tell us that Nick has a walnut-sized hole in his left jaw tissue with bone protruding into the hole. He was unable to do the surgery and just cleaned up the area. He called today a "Peek and Shriek". You've got to love surgeons. Some of them have no clue that they are talking about another human being.
He said he will reschedule the surgery but will need to take Nick's "push up muscle" and use it in his mouth. He also said that Nick will never be able to stick his tongue out, up, or down.

I cried when I was alone. Nick's speech and eating will never be the same. I find myself hating Brandon right now. I am also eating my words about him "not messing up our kissing".

We brought Nick home with us. He is sore and disgusted.

Saturday, February 19, 2005

Nick has been using a large syringe to suck up his cans of food and force them into the feeding tube. The more he is able to take in that way, the less he has to be attached to the pump. It also allows him to "eat" meals with us at the table.

I spent Kenzie's nap time reading our health insurance handbook. I keep getting Determination of Benefits that aren't being paid, yet I haven't received any bills. I tend to be very anal when it comes to budgeting and finances. I now find myself not worrying about it as much. It's just too time consuming to worry about something that I have no control over and Nick's needs. His recovery is so much more important. We will find a way to pay everything that needs to be paid when the time comes. Luckily, Nick has always been awesome about saving his sick and vacation time. We should continue to receive a paycheck for at least another six months. Hopefully by then I might be able to go back to work.

Brandon called today to see how Nick's surgery went yesterday. I told him what happened, and that Nick and I are having a tough time handling the news. Brandon barely spoke to me.

Tuesday, February 22, 2005

Nick had a pre-op appointment with Dr. Case today. He has surgery scheduled for this Friday.

I decided to make a pouch for Nick's feeding tube. It hangs awkwardly so he is always holding it when walks to keep it from pulling, and to prevent it from getting caught on something. I sewed several pouches that Velcro over his belt and so far, they seem to work.

Tonight, we had an unbelievable surprise. Nick's twin, Nolan, called to tell us that some of Nick's family and friends held a gathering in his honor. They raised $4937.00! Nick almost cried. They are planning on using the money to purchase a laptop computer and a year of internet service. This is so exciting!! Nick will be able to communicate with distant family and friends when he is recovering from surgeries! It's been way too long since he has been able to speak to anyone, but at least we can see his whiteboard. I am so happy for him!

Kenzie, Nick, and I put on CMT tonight and danced together in the sunroom. We also played with a flashlight and Kenzie's glow in the dark pajamas. It's the little things that mean so much.

Friday February 25, 2005

Gloria, Nick, Dad, and I went to the hospital for Nick's 12:40pm surgery. Once again, I got to watch him get intubated. It is NOT a pretty sight.

Dr. Case came to us at 6:15pm to say that he was able to snip Nick's left pectoral muscle under his nipple then push it up, still attached, through his neck. He had to make a relief cut on the left side of his neck to make it fit. He then pushed it across the hole in his chin and attached it to the two molars on the right side of Nick's mouth. He then covered the relief cut on Nick's neck with a skin graft from his thigh. Dr. Case couldn't remove the external fixator and replace it with a titanium plate because the pectoral muscle was too bulky.

At 8pm, they let Gloria and I see Nick in recovery, and he joked with us. He teased, on his whiteboard, that he didn't know which one of us was his mother. Gloria and the recovery nurse got quite a kick out of it. Me, not so much. He hit a little too close to home with his comment and the old and ragged way I feel lately.

Nick looks good yet he is extremely swollen with a softball sized bulge on the left side of his neck. He has two drains coming out of him: one from his neck and a second from his chest.

It is Dr. Case's hope that the pectoral muscle will attach itself to the surrounding tissues, then grow its own blood supply and innervation to essentially become the new floor to Nick's mouth. Now, we pray.

Saturday, February 26, 2005

    Dad, Gloria, and I went to see Nick. His face lit up when I walked in. It made me feel so good! I love him so much. He did well with surgery and has such an awesome attitude.

    It's hard to believe that this is the same man who used to cringe at having his teeth cleaned. He was always an easy cleaning too because he takes such good care of his teeth. To have him cringe at that, but be so tough with this, it's truly remarkable.

    He told us about a medical student who came in to check him early this morning before Dr. Case did his rounds. The medical student removed Nick's bandages and checked everything over then rebandaged him.

    When Dr. Case came in a bit later, with a group of students, he was teaching them about Nick's case. He asked them a question, and the student who was there earlier was quick to answer. Dr. Case seemed impressed until Nick told him, "He should know, he looked at me earlier."

    Dr. Case questioned the young man and was very upset with him. Apparently, though it is a teaching hospital, the students are not to check his patients without him present. Poor Nick had his bandages removed more than was necessary.

    Dad, Gloria, and I stayed with Nick until 7pm. I hate to have him in the hospital, though it gives me a little break from doing his care, it also keeps us from Kenzie. We both despise that. Thank God for my mom. Kenzie loves being with her.

Monday, February 28, 2005

    Nick is doing well but is in a lot of pain. His blood sugar is 342. It should be in the low to mid 100s. I'm very worried. Gloria decided to spend the night at the hospital, so I headed home in the afternoon to spend time with Kenzie.

    My mom came to spend the night with Kenzie and me. It was good to be able to talk to her alone for a change. I love having Gloria here, but I seldom get to talk to anyone without her being there. Sometimes, I just want to talk to my own parents alone.

    I am so freaked out about Nick's neck and chest. It looks so painful, and I can't help but think that they destroyed a perfectly good part of him in the hope of fixing another. His strong chest has always been a part of him that I have admired. I love snuggling up against him in bed with my head on his chest. That will never be the same. One more thing that I mourn along with his beautiful mouth and kisses. When I feel like this, I just remind myself that I could be mourning ALL of him. I am very lucky he's still here. I just pray this surgery works.

Tuesday, March 1, 2005

I shoveled eight inches of snow, fed the dogs, and did laundry before Dad came over to plow this morning. Mom stayed with Kenzie while Dad drove me to the hospital to get Nick and Gloria.

We sat around until 3:30 pm before they released him. He was so tired and sore it was awful.

We got Nick home and into the hospital bed in the living room, but he just couldn't get comfortable. He was very cranky and snippy. Kenzie was whining at the same time, and I just wanted to crawl in a corner and cry. It is so hard not to get frustrated with his attitude, but I know poor Nick is in a lot of pain, so I just have to bear with it. He goes from seemingly okay to ornery in the blink of an eye. It's hard to know which Nick I am dealing with.

Thursday, March 3, 2005

Our niece, Eliza, was born today!! Geena and Nolan are thrilled with their 7lb, 4oz, healthy baby girl. We are so happy for them! Gloria, Nick, Kenzie, and I posed for a "Hurray!" photo with all of us in pink shirts and sent it to them.

On the home front, Nick is still really hurting. I'm a nervous wreck when it comes to changing bandages on his skin graft. It's so delicate and intricate, I don't want to hurt anything. There are two layers of bandages, one that protects the bandage and one against the graft. The thigh is much the same except the second bandage is against the very raw areas on his leg.

I still need to clean his external fixator pins and the proximity of them to his neck makes it very difficult to get in there without disturbing anything.

Cary and Brandon visited tonight. Brandon is still on desk duty since the accident. We all sat together in the living room awkwardly. Cary and I were able to get away from the guys for a couple of minutes to chat in the kitchen while we got drinks. I feel so bad for her.

I miss having just our own little family at home. I love Gloria, and I am beyond grateful for her, but I miss being able to talk to Nick alone. The fact that we're still sleeping in the living room, and everyone basically walks through our bedroom, does not help the situation at all.

Thursday, March 10, 2005

    We went for Nick's post-op visit with Dr. Case today. It went well and he cracked us up when he examined Nick. As he went to take a look, he just stood there and didn't move. He then grinned and told Nick that he was waiting for him to get his "fricking hand out of the way". We just didn't expect that from a young surgeon who wears a bow tie.

    We told Dr. Case that Nick has been losing weight. At the time of the accident, he weighed one hundred and thirty-one pounds. Before the last surgery he weighed one hundred twenty-five pounds. Now he is one hundred twenty pounds. Dr. Case recommended that we increase Nick's cans of food from six to eight cans a day.

    When we got home, I sewed Nick some "turtlenecks" that close with Velcro. They will hold his bandage in place on his neck skin graft. They are less bulky and will allow for more movement and comfort. The problem is, he has very limited movement with the pectoral muscle in his neck. It strains due to the bulk of it, much like having a pulled, tight muscle. He can't turn his head much, nor can he look up.

Saturday, March 12, 2005

    We had more snow overnight. John and Krista came over to plow and shovel for me. Krista fed the dogs too. My Dad has been doing it, but he fell yesterday, and no one told me. I hate asking for help, and even more so knowing Dad fell. Krista and John have enough of their own stuff to do.
    Brandon came to visit. He still won't talk. I wonder if that will ever change. I don't know if he feels guilty or if he's afraid to say something because his lawyer told him not to. Either way, there are plenty of things going on in the world, he doesn't have to talk about the accident. Since Nick is able to speak now, you would think that things would be getting better with Brandon, not worse.
    I'm so tired from constantly worrying about Nick. He still has the hole under his chin and today there was bloody discharge when I removed his bandage to do his care. I don't know what is "normal" for this type of surgery nor what I should be seeing. Honestly, I think this is a whole new type of case even for his doctor.
    I feel bad because I know that Nick wants to drink so badly. I made lemon swabs for his throat today in hopes of making him comfortable. This stinks!

Sunday, March 13, 2005

I woke up this morning and got very concerned. Nick's weight is down to one hundred thirteen pounds. He is so weak and exhausted. I asked my mom to bring over my dad's blood sugar monitor. Nick tested his blood sugar, and it was four hundred seventy-one.

Something needed to be done so I called Nick's regular physician. He wasn't available and the doctor on call said that he wouldn't deal with the blood sugar issue so we should go to the Emergency Room. I called Krista. She works at our local hospital so she said she would go with us.

When we got to the Emergency Room at 1:30pm, Nick's blood sugar level was four hundred forty-eight, but all his other labs were good. They gave him insulin and 2000cc of sodium chloride through an IV. He felt much better.

Since the doctor covering for his general practitioner wanted nothing to do with him, the hospitalist there wouldn't admit him nor release him. The hospital wanted to load him in an ambulance and send him to Harris Hospital.

Thankfully, I was able to reach his Trauma Surgeon at Harris Hospital and he agreed to take responsibility for Nick. He gave them instructions, told me that our visiting nurse would have a sliding scale for insulin, and that she would teach me how to inject Nick tomorrow morning.

We got home from the hospital at 9pm. Apparently, Nick's weight loss and frequent urinating was because of diabetes. The Emergency Room Hospitalist told us that the Diabetes could be trauma induced. My question is, why didn't Dr. Case pick up on that instead of increasing Nick's food which is apparently high in carbohydrates?

Friday, March 18, 2005

Things have quieted down a bit. I am doing Nick's blood sugar testing and insulin, as needed, four times a day. The injections are fairly easy for me since they are the same type of injections that I used for our invitro-fertilization.

Nick's regular physician, Dr. Dee, felt bad that the doctor covering for him didn't help him. He has me calling him with Nick's blood sugars every three days.

I went to get my hair cut today and was surprised to see a poster on the wall. A benefit is being held for Nick tomorrow and they were selling tickets there. We had no idea. People continue to amaze me.

When I got home and told Nick, he told me that he wants me to go to the benefit to say, "Thank you". We both got teary eyed thinking about how lucky we are to have all these wonderful people in our lives. I will go to the benefit with Krista and John tomorrow night. I have to say that leaving Nick and facing the questions that are bound to be asked without him, makes me very nervous.

We received the laptop from Nick's family today. I set it up for Nick tonight and got it hooked up to the internet. It's awesome! He truly enjoyed emailing his family and friends. Though he can talk now, he's hard to understand and gets sore talking for any length of time. The laptop is going to be great for him!

Saturday, March 19, 2005

Krista and John picked me up tonight to go to the benefit at Spades Bar. The turnout was amazing! The men who own the bar are coworkers of Nick's, and they did a great job with everything.

Kyle and Brandon had worked hard on selling tickets and getting donations of raffle prizes. There were so many familiar, and unfamiliar, faces. The bar was so packed that the excess crowd filtered out onto the back deck. They had heaters out there to keep people warm too.

They had received huge raffle prizes: large screen TVs, DVD players, a porch swing, an oriental rug, gas grill, tools, die cast models, booze, baskets, etc. We stayed for the raffle, and I was amused watching Kyle call off the winners. That guy has a magnetic personality and is simply just a great guy.

I couldn't say "thank you" enough as I chatted with people. I also couldn't wait to tell Nick all about it when I got home.

I tried to remember every little detail and every name when I told Nick. We both cried. Thank God for good people. This is all very humbling. I think Nick has cried more over the good-hearted gestures of the people around us than he has over the accident.

Sunday, March 20, 2005

    We were completely overwhelmed today. Kyle came over with a DVD of last night's benefit, almost ten thousand dollars in cash, and a new DVD/VCR player. Unbelievable! Kyle set up the DVD player for us and we all watched the movie. Nick's face lit up seeing his friends on the DVD and pointing them out to us.

    When I stop to think how I have been able to focus on Nick and not money and our budget, I realize it's because I have faith that we'll all be okay. It's because of God, and the people around us, that we are okay. I haven't worked in three months, nor has Nick. All we can do is say "thank you" and let people know how much we truly appreciate them.

Sunday, March 27, 2005, ~ Easter

The Easter Bunny brought Kenzie a wagon and hid four dozen eggs for her to find. She was so animated during her hunt! She thought of great places that the Easter bunny didn't too! I made a mental note for next year.

Gloria, Nick, Kenzie, and I met my family at our church for 9am mass, then we all went to Krista and John's for Easter brunch afterwards.

Kenzie and Gwen had a blast playing together. As I watched Nick, I felt sick inside. He tries to put up a good front, but I can see how sad he is not to be able to eat and play with us. Feeding himself through a feeding tube and not being able to get close to anyone for fear of hurting the skin grafts has got to be disheartening.

I pray that he'll get to a point where he can have a happy life. I love him so much.

Friday, April 1, 2005

    Nick's speech therapist came today. Since he hasn't had any leaks in over a week, Dr. Case gave the okay. She did a swallow study and had Nick try applesauce, pudding, thickened apple juice, and thickened water. I was so happy, I almost cried. The therapist feels that Nick may never eat solid foods again, but I'm grateful that he should be able to get rid of the feeding tube eventually. I pray she's wrong about the solid foods.
    Nick is still so bothered by memories of the abuse he received at the hands of the nurses in the hospital at Christmas time. He decided to write a letter to the hospital detailing the abuse. He has no intention of pressing charges, or suing, but I asked him to hold off sending it to the hospital until his surgeries are over. I'm fearful that they'll seek retribution.
    Today was a rollercoaster of emotion. It was a very good reason for us to go out for sugar-free ice cream tonight!

Saturday, April 2, 2005

When I did Nick's wound care today, I found a leaky area under the front of his chin. After one day of liquids, he must stop eating by mouth again. He had done so well today too. He drank four cans of food and had some pudding before we got the word to stop.

One of Nick's friends called tonight. Nick told him the whole story about the accident. I want to vomit every time I think about it, let alone the fact that Nick wants to hunt again. I can't seem to get the thought of him gurgling on the walkie talkie out of my head. Though I wasn't there, that sound haunts me. It's bizarre how the mind works.

I was so hopeful that he wouldn't want to hunt again, but once he knew that none of this was his fault, his attitude changed entirely. That scares me to death.

Friday, April 8, 2005

Nick and I went to our local hospital for a modified barium swallow study. They found that his epiglottis is not working and that he also has two leaks. It is so discouraging.

We met Jim, a registered nurse in the Emergency Room there at the hospital. He told us that he was in the E.R. on the night of the accident and had helped with Nick's care. Jim told us that everyone was so busy working on Nick that night there were no extra hands. Jim kept yelling out that he needed someone to hold a clamp for him. The next thing he knew, Nick was reaching up to hold the clamp. Jim looked at Nick today and said, "You're one tough son of a bitch!".

When we got home, Nick decided to work on the battery terminals of our camper. For some reason, he didn't wear his feeding tube pouch. He sat on a milk crate, cleaning the terminals, and when he got up, his feeding tube got caught on the crate. Let's just say that a lot of expletives came rolling out of his mouth. All I could picture was a trip to the emergency room to reinsert his feeding tube and stomach contents leaking everywhere. Thank God that didn't happen.

Tonight, I was kneeling beside Nick doing his care, and I burst into tears. All I could think of was how many times I have given him heck through the years for stealing cookies from my Christmas cookie bins. Now, he may never eat them again. How stupid I was to get irritated over something so insignificant. I pray he will eat eventually.

Saturday, April 9, 2005

    I went to Cary's baby shower today. Her family did a fantastic job planning it!

    It was a beautiful shower, but I felt so awkward. So many people asked about Nick. I couldn't admit how bad things really are. I didn't want to ruin her shower. She's my best friend. Her life has changed so much too. I just kept telling people, "He's hanging in there".

    Cary got a lot of wonderful gifts today. I just hope she enjoyed the day like she should have. She's going to be a great mom and she deserves the very best!

Monday, April 11, 2005

    Gloria flew home today after three and a half months. I cried when she left. We have so much ahead of us and though my parents are right down the road, there was a certain sense of security with her here. I knew I always had back up when I needed it, or a shoulder to cry on. Her experience as a nurse was also reassuring when I have questioned if we should call the doctor. To be honest, I'm a bit scared to face the next few months without her.

    Since Nick got home from the hospital in January, he and I have slept on the hospital and twin bed in the living room and Gloria has slept in our bed. Tonight, was the first time we slept in our own bed together. I am petrified to roll into his external fixator or his skin graft. It's going to be a long night.

Thursday, April 14, 2005

An ear, nose and throat specialist was recommended to Nick today when we went to see Dr. Case. Nick has very thick secretions that gag him, and the specialist could also address the inactive epiglottis. First, though, he wants him to have a barium x-ray.

Brandon came over when we got home. He told us that he's being charged with negligent hunting and reckless endangerment. Nick assured him that he has no intention of pressing charges and will not help the prosecution. The state filed those charges, not Nick.

Though I don't want anything to happen to Brandon legally, I don't agree with Nick. He keeps saying that he won't be judge and jury for his friend. Of course not. But Brandon should not be allowed to have a gun, ever again, in my opinion.

Saturday, April 16, 2005

Back in January, when my mom talked to us about going camping this spring, that possibility seemed unimaginable. Well, Mom was right! My parents were in the campsite next to ours last night. Thankfully, our motorhome made it possible to have a getaway.

We had all the comforts of home since the campground had water, sewer, and electricity at our site. I packed everything that I needed to do Nick's care, so I was hopeful we could relax and enjoy some time away.

Kenzie hung out with my parents last night so Nick and I could go to his coworker's retirement party. We were completely thrown off when Nick got a standing ovation for being there. He was so happy to see his friends. He repeated the story of the accident numerous times. His friends, like me, marveled at his fortitude.

Well, so much for camping. We had fun this morning, fishing with Kenzie and my parents, but by this afternoon Kenzie was running a 104-degree fever. I called her pediatrician and found she has a case of Roseola.

We left the campground and came home to be able to soak her in a luke-warm tub. I unpacked the camper and put everything away. At least we had a short time away.

Monday, April 18, 2005

    Nick and I went to his general physician, Dr. Dee, for a presurgical exam. Although I have had all of Nick's hospital records forwarded to his office, and I talk to him every week regarding Nick's blood sugars, he has not physically seen Nick since the accident.

    Dr. Dee sat at his desk with his back to Nick for almost the entire appointment. He questioned me about the hospital, surgeries, and blood sugars then turned to Nick, who still has his external fixator on his face, and said, "So, I understand, Mr. Joseph, that you were shot in the abdomen?" Are you kidding me?!?! Sure, the external fixator is a new fad that people are wearing! Did he not listen at all to everything that I had JUST told him?

    That man is a total moron! We need to find Nick a new physician.

Friday, April 22, 2005

    Nick and I went for his barium x-rays and swallow study. They saw no leaks and his epiglottis is working! We stopped on the way home for Nick's first iced coffee. French vanilla was his favorite just prior to the accident. He was thrilled!

    I'm concerned with his external fixator though. All three times that I did his care today, he has pus coming out of scar tissue by the third pin. Supposedly he will have the fixator removed on Kenzie's second birthday next month. Hopefully he can hold out until then. Either way, I put a call in to Dr. Case to let him know.

    The nausea, abdominal and lower back pain that I've been having are really starting to get to me. I feel horrible from the time I get up until the time I go to bed. It keeps me up at night too. If this keeps up, I am going to have to schedule an appointment with my doctor.

Wednesday, April 27, 2005

I called my mom at 6am and asked her to take me to the Emergency Room. I was in a lot of abdominal and lower back pain all night and this morning. More pain than I had been having.

The doctors ran a bunch of bloodwork, did exams, and a CT scan. I have a ruptured ovarian cyst. Everything else looks good thank God. The fluid that got released when it ruptured could have been what was causing the extra nausea too. At least now I know I'm okay.

When I got home, I found two state police sergeants here questioning Nick about the accident. Neither were acting very friendly toward Nick, and they explained that they were doing an internal affairs investigation on Brandon. If they are doing an investigation on Brandon, why act so stiff with my husband?

After a few minutes, I recognized one of the officers as a patient of mine from a previous office. When I said, "Well, hello Lou Lindy!" he took one look at me and grinned.

Thankfully, that lightened the foreboding atmosphere in the room as we caught up on each other's families and he proceeded to question Nick. He really is a nice guy, and I know he has a job to do, but knowing me should not have been a precursor to being nice to Nick.

Sunday, May 1, 2005

We celebrated Kenzie's second birthday today. Her real birthday is tomorrow, but Nick is having surgery, so we won't be seeing much of her.

We sang happy birthday to her when she woke up. She helped me to set her Winnie the Pooh themed birthday table and got very excited. I had made and decorated a Winnie the Pooh cake yesterday and I was pretty excited about how it came out. There were ten of us for pizza, cake, ice cream and snacks.

Brandon and Cary did not join us this year. They were blessed with a beautiful baby girl, Elizabeth, four days ago. I am thrilled for them, especially Cary. She deserves some true happiness. I know snuggling that peanut will make her days ten times happier!

We had a lot of laughs and Gwen helped Kenzie blow out her candles. Our guests left at 7pm except for my parents, who stayed until 8pm. They took Kenzie home with them for a sleepover so we can leave early tomorrow for Nick's surgery. It breaks our hearts that we won't be with her on her real birthday, but at least we got to celebrate together today.

Monday, May 2, 2005

    Since Gloria isn't staying with us anymore, my parents took care of Kenzie and Gwen so Krista and I could go to the hospital with Nick. Though it's not necessary for someone to come with me, I can't explain how comforting it is to have the company, especially while Nick's in surgery and I'm worrying. Krista never fails to make me laugh when I am stressing. I don't think she realizes how much she means to me.

    We left for the hospital at 4:10am and I went to Pre-Op once again with Nick. His three and one quarter hour surgery ended up taking four- and three-quarter hours. Dr. Case placed a full titanium reconstruction plate in his jaw with nine screws. He removed Nick's external fixator and wired his mouth shut again.

    Krista and I went to Friendly's for lunch then waited for Nick to go up to his room. When he got up there, he started vomiting. +His head was wrapped up like a mummy. He was miserable, the poor guy. He told me to come home to Kenzie, but Krista and I stayed until 7:30pm. We just couldn't leave him like that, so we waited until the vomiting subsided.

    When I got home, Mom and Kenzie were waiting for me. I got to snuggle Kenzie for a bit on her birthday. That was much needed.

Wednesday, May 4, 2005

    Nick called me this morning and said, "You've got one good looking husband." That statement tickled me. After seeing the pain that he was in yesterday, it was nice to hear him joking around. Thank God for my career in dental hygiene, listening to patients talk with their mouth full, I can understand him talking with his mouth wired shut!
    My mom watched Kenzie while dad and I went to the hospital. Nick looks great! His teeth still hurt but he feels much better. He asked me to kiss his lips. It was the first time in four and a half months due to the external fixator. Sadly, he can no longer feel his lower lip. The realization has so many implications. He won't be able to tell when food is coming out of his mouth, when his lips are chapped, and kissing will never be the same. I am heartbroken for him.

Thursday, May 5, 2005

Nick got his jaw unwired this morning. Dad and I went to get him, but we had to wait for Dr. Bennett, the oral surgeon, to check him before he was released. It wasn't until 3pm that they informed us that Dr. Bennett wasn't coming. We had just sat there for hours for nothing. This was the second time that we had to wait for Dr. Bennett but at least the first time he eventually came. They did release Nick though.

We stopped at the pharmacy on the way home to get Nick's post-surgery prescriptions. When we got home, I realized that one of the prescriptions was a capsule. You CAN'T use a capsule in a feeding tube! They know he can only have liquid in his feeding tube. He isn't allowed to put anything in his mouth until he is healed from the surgery for goodness sakes! I ran back to the pharmacy to return it and get a liquid form.

Once I got home, I also found that the pill they called in for his diabetes can't be crushed either. I called the pharmacist and he said that I would have to call Dr. Dee tomorrow. I broke down and cried. Why can't these doctors get their act straight? Especially the surgeons who are dealing with Nick and prescribing the medications. They should know better!

Nick and I are back to sleeping in the living room again. The hospital bed is more comfortable for him since he can elevate his head to help with the throbbing pain.

Sunday, May 9, 2005, ~ Mother's Day

Nick's chin has been leaking for three days now. Dr. Case told us that we just need to be patient, but this morning, I discovered a new hole in his chin. I cried my eyes out. This poor man.

John came over to mow the lawn and trim this afternoon. That is no small job with the raised bed garden, playhouse, house, and garage to trim around. I really appreciated it. I had not had the chance to get out there yet.

My Mom made Sunday dinner and brought it here so we could all be together. Our family is so awesome. I felt bad having Mom cook on Mother's Day, but she said she was just happy we are all together.

They all share in our grief over Nick's chin too, so we all worked hard to lighten the atmosphere. Of course, Gwen and Kenzie always provide a bit of comic relief.

Monday, May 9, 2005

    Nick and I went to Dr. Bennett's office. He's the oral maxillofacial surgeon who saw Nick while he was in the hospital. He took a panorex x-ray and recommended that we make an appointment to have the orthodontic brackets and arch wires removed that had helped to wire Nick shut after surgery.

    I called Dr. Case to let him know that the hole in Nick's chin is larger today. I also made new "slings" for his chin. The old ones hooked on his external fixator; these hook on his ears.

    I am scared shitless over Nick's chin. It appears to be a fairly deep hole again. I thought the pectoral muscle was supposed to fill that in. I just pray that Nick heals.

Tuesday, May 10, 2005

Nick and I went to Dr. Case's office today. He was surprised to see where the hole is under Nick's chin and was disappointed. He does feel that it will heal though. It looks much bigger today. I am having trouble believing him.

Brandon, Cary, and Elizabeth visited tonight. Cary calls to check on us, but we never get a call from Brandon. I got to hold Elizabeth for a while. She is adorable, and you can't beat that new baby smell.

I'm a wreck about Nick's chin. That hole just keeps growing. Please God, don't let the pectoral muscle surgery have been for nothing.

Wednesday, May 11, 2005

Windy, Nick's visiting nurse, came for her weekly visit today. It's always so nice to chit chat with her. That woman has such a perky disposition, she always brightens our day.

When she left, Nick and I took Kenzie to the pediatrician for her two-year-old checkup. She has grown three and three-quarter inches in the last six months! She is doing great!

After supper, I did Nick's care as usual. I freaked when I saw how big his wound is now. It's one and one quarter inches long by three quarters of an inch wide. I called Dr. Case's office and was told to call tomorrow for an appointment.

I cried. I am so scared and so is Nick. The wound looks terrible. It's red, and raw, almost meaty. What if the pectoral flap surgery was nothing but a waste?

Thursday, May 12, 2005

When I did Nick's care this morning, he confided to me that he is scared shitless that he'll end up in the ICU again and be mistreated. I don't blame him at all. This mess is exactly why I didn't want him to write a letter to the hospital until he is fixed. That would just add fuel to the fire.

I called Dr. Case and he saw Nick this morning. He isn't happy but recommended that we "just watch it". Seriously, just watch it. I have been watching it. I have been watching it get bigger!

Nick had a lot of shooting pain in his left jaw today. I wonder if it is stress related or trauma related? One more thing that we'll have to watch. That poor guy can't catch a break.

Tuesday, May 17, 2005

Brandon and Cary visited today. The police union collected over six hundred dollars for us. It's been almost six months since the accident and these generous people haven't forgotten about us. It's heartwarming.

Nick also saw a diabetes counselor, Nancy, who is an APRN. We learned more from her in the one-hour visit than we did in several visits with Dr. Dee. She is very professional and caring. I'm so glad Krista recommended her!

Nolan, Geena, and Eliza are flying here tomorrow. I pulled out a bunch of Kenzie's baby items including her pack and play. Kenzie was so excited when she got off the phone with Geena. She said, "Auntie say me me can hold baby on lap."

I've been feeling shaky and nauseous again. I hope it's not another ovarian cyst.

Thursday, May 19, 2005

I was nervous and excited for Nolan, Geena, and Eliza to visit. There's so much going on here, I wasn't sure I could be a good hostess. What I needed to remember is that they are family and that they understand.

We finally got to meet Eliza and she's adorable! She has a strong desire to be swaddled and I enjoy watching Nolan do it. Her little rosy cheeks and big eyes won our hearts right away.

Nolan helped Nick with the dogs today which left time for Geena and me to talk. It has been way too long since I've seen her. I think this visit is going to be good for all of us. And, Kenzie, of course, loves little Eliza.

Saturday, May 20, 2005

Kenzie woke up vomiting this morning. Will the ongoing list of crap never end? The poor kid is so sick.

I'm worried that Eliza, who is only two and a half months old, or Nick, will catch it. Wouldn't you know that the one year we decide to get the flu vaccine, because of Nick, she catches the flu. I know the vaccine only covers certain strains, but good gravy.

I'm trying to keep Kenzie away from everyone but with six of us in the house, it's not easy. I had her set up on her little Elmo couch in the sunroom with a stainless-steel bowl on the side of her all day. I am so glad that I thought to put a waterproof pad on the Elmo couch because at one point, Kenzie had poop come out her diaper and go straight up her back. What a mess!

Kyle took Nick and Nolan saltwater fishing for part of the day on his boat. It was a big treat for Nolan who never gets out on the ocean. It was a big treat for Nick too as he loves to be with his twin and his best friend.

They had a good time, but Nick got very tired and came home to nap all afternoon. Later we all chatted and relaxed.

Tuesday, May 24, 2005

    Nolan, Geena, and Eliza flew home today. As soon as they left, I started vomiting. Thank God it held off until after they left!
    Dad went to Dr. Case's with Nick. Dr. Case wants to do more exams to decide on future surgeries. We are totally disgusted.
    Nick took care of Kenzie later today and she gave him a hard time because she's not used to him helping any more. Nick is so upset. He's always been such a big part of her life. He really wants to get back on track.
    To top it all off, our washing machine exploded oil out the back and bottom today. I felt so horrible but needed to clean it up. I didn't want Nick straining to move it or risk hurting his jaw. What next!

Friday, May 27, 2005

    I only slept about two hours last night. I had terrible anxiety, heartburn, and rapid heartbeat. I called my gynecologist because I had just started a new medication and I wasn't sure if that could be the cause. She recommended that I head straight to the Emergency Room because she was concerned that I might have a pulmonary embolism.

    My mom took me to the Emergency Room where I had a CT scan, EKG, and a battery of bloodwork. They diagnosed me with esophageal reflux, probably made worse by the stress, gave me medication, and sent me home. Thank God it's nothing else!

Sunday, May 29, 2005

    My parents, Krista's family, Nick, Kenzie, and I went to the zoo today. I was so excited to go. I thought that it would be a stress reliever.

    We barely walked two hundred feet into the zoo when Nick's feeding tube valve opened and emptied stomach contents all over his clothes. Thankfully we were near the rest room, so Nick went straight in there. The poor guy tried to clean up as best as he could, but he smelled like vomit all day. I can only imagine how humiliated he felt. It ruined the day for him and me. I could see the stress and upset of it in his eyes and spent the day just waiting for the other shoe to drop.

    At least the kids had fun. They both love the elephants and giraffes. We had lunch on the picnic tables and came home this afternoon. Nick headed right upstairs to shower then I did laundry. Today was a zoo trip that we will never forget.

Tuesday, June 14, 2005

I took a bit of a break from writing in my journal to just enjoy the little things. In the last two weeks, we have had the chance to camp twice and finally relaxed a bit.

Kenzie had her first ride on a school bus when we were at the first campground. The owner was a kind man who also drives school bus for the school that Kenzie will attend in a couple of years. He took us on his afternoon ride to pick up a load of kindergarteners. Those cute little faces brightened my day and Kenzie absolutely loved it!

Nick met with a new speech therapist. She gave him a sheet of words to practice pronouncing: tight, light, sight, bright, etc. His frustration is palpable. I can't blame him. He cannot move his tongue so relearning how to speak without it is beyond difficult.

The second campground we went to was near Dr. Case's office. He continues to tell us to be patient and wait for healing. He is getting less and less believable with each visit.

Today, Nick and I went to Dr. Bennett's office. He used IV sedation to remove the arch bars on Nick's teeth. He feels that some of the exposed bone under Nick's chin is dead and that the tissue will not heal to cover the now exposed titanium reconstructive plate. He hopes that once Nick is totally done with surgeries and healed, that Nick might be able to move his tongue a bit. I will take that bit of hope!

Wednesday, June 15, 2005

    Today was my first day back to work! My boss brought in his daughter's Barbie tricycle for Kenzie and my coworker presented me with a beautiful lap quilt that she made. I had three patients this morning and four this afternoon. My coworkers were beyond supportive, and it was a good day.
    When I got home, I learned that nurse Windy brought Kenzie a t-shirt when she came to do Nick's care today. Windy just returned from a trip to Spain. How sweet of her to think of Kenzie while she was away!
    Tomorrow, Nick, and I will head to the hospital for his head and neck arteriogram. Dr. Case wants to see if the pectoral muscle is settling in and growing blood supply. We are seriously in need of good news for Nick.

Thursday, June 23, 2005

Nick and I went to his appointment with Dr. Case. He doesn't know what to do with Nick, so he recommended one more month of healing.

The issue we have is that Nick is not actually healing. More and more of his reconstruction plate is showing. It looks like the tissue is peeling away from it. I am back to stuffing sterile, saline soaked gauze under his chin while I watch more and more of the bone begin to show. I dread doing his care each of the three times that I do it every day because I never know what I am going to find.

This feeling of being in limbo is so frustrating for both of us. Nick wants to get back to work but that can't happen until he is healed, and the feeding tube is gone. How could the Department of Corrections let him back to work like this? Not with inmate contact, that's for sure.

Saturday, July 2, 2005

    Nick's sister, Melanie, and her husband, Joe, are here visiting. They drove out a few days ago and having them here is wonderful!

    We took them to the beach to visit my parents at their camper. Watching Melanie interact with Kenzie was priceless. Kenzie had her little ladybug bikini and cover up on while she played in the sand. She and Melanie built a sandcastle with a moat and Kenzie loved it.

    Joe, who does not usually show his soft side, was beyond sweet with Kenzie. He had her riding on his shoulders as they walked the beach. I love these two people and truly appreciate having them here.

    It's good for Nick to have Joe here too. I know he misses them all and having a guy to chat with is always nice for him. We are really going to miss them when they leave tomorrow.

Saturday, July 9, 2005

Nick and I have very different feelings about Brandon. We were contacted a month ago by a victim's advocate. She asked if there was anything she could do for us. She has been a liaison between Nick and the detectives when trying to get Nick's cell phone, gun, walkie talkie, and hunting clothes back. But, until Brandon is sentenced, Nick can't get anything back.

Nick has always said that he would not speak against Brandon. If the state chooses to punish Brandon, that's up to them. He will have no part in it.

The victim's advocate told Nick and me that we have a right to be heard in court at Brandon's sentencing. If we choose not to talk, we can write a letter.

At this point, Brandon has reached a plea bargain. The state has dropped the reckless endangerment charge and he will plead guilty to negligent hunting.

I, personally, do not feel that Brandon should have a gun. As a police officer, he needs to have good decision-making skills and quickly at that. He was in a prone position, aimed, and shot Nick thinking he was a deer. A deer that weighed one hundred thirty-one pounds, and wore orange clothing in the white, snowy woods. A deer, on a tote road, where his friend was supposed to be waiting for him.

That act made an emotional mess of Brandon. What if he makes the wrong decision again? What if he shoots another innocent person? What if he's called to a domestic disturbance and a child runs out and startles him? Or, what if he's afraid to shoot when he needs to because he now has self-doubt? He could get himself killed. Where would Cary and their little girl be then?

Nick doesn't want to write a letter. He doesn't want me to write one either. To be honest, I have let Nick take the lead on how we deal with Brandon because he was the one who was injured. But the reality is, our whole family has been affected by that accident.

I really want to write a letter to let Brandon know my fears. I have to give this some thought. Part of me wonders if we'll ever hear from Brandon again after his court date, whether I write a letter, or not.

Sunday, July 10, 2005

Nick, Kenzie, and I went to a college graduation party for Kyle's wife today. She graduated from the same Dental Hygiene program that I did. I am very happy for her.

I couldn't believe the comments people made to us about the rumors that were circulating right after the accident. Some people heard that Brandon shot Nick because he and I were having an affair. That was beyond ridiculous! We dated in high school for a short time but there is nothing between us than friendship nor has there been in almost twenty years.

Others thought that Nick was walking in front of Brandon when Brandon slipped and shot him. That would have been impossible considering the projectile went in the right side of Nick's jaw and came out the left.

All this talk left Nick wondering what Brandon told the police. He never has told Nick what happened.

Deer on a Tote Road

Tuesday, July 12, 2005

    We saw the police report for the accident for the first time yesterday. I was nauseous just reading it. Nick, who had refused to let me write a letter until then, finally agreed. Of course, now that the plea bargain has been made, my letter will do nothing other than let Brandon know how I feel.

    Nick and I went to court for Brandon's sentencing today. He pleaded no contest to the charge of negligent hunting. He got a one-year suspended sentence, eighteen months of probation, and a four hundred dollar fine. He must forfeit his hunting license for ten years then take a hunting course to get it back.

    Only the judge and Brandon saw my letter. I did not read it out loud. The judge was very nice about my letter and the difficulties that Nick and I have been through. I knew that the letter would have no bearing on the proceedings, but I needed Brandon to know my fears. My only hope is that Brandon thinks about it and makes sure he is in fact fit for duty not only physically but emotionally.

Monday, July 18, 2005

Nick and I went to the State Police Barracks to get his belongings. We came home and emptied four boxes of blood covered items. There was SO much dark, dried, blood. They had cut off all his clothes except his boot laces. There were two notes from him that he had written that night. One said, "Kenzie and Yve, I love you." The other said, "I have a wife, Yve, and a daughter, Kenzie. I want to live another day."

I can't express how much I hurt. The fear he had of dying that night had to have been horrific. I was touched that he wanted to live another day, for us. I cried so hard. I methodically cleaned the hard, brown, dried blood from his cell phone and walkie talkie. The walkie talkie he had gurgled in to. The cell phone that he misdialed when he tried to call 911. The tears just wouldn't stop. Thank God he wanted to live.

Tonight, I used a mouth mirror to look inside Nick's mouth for the first time. He has a metal "X" bar on the visible bone behind his lower front teeth. I don't see how that is ever going to heal. I am scared and worried. I just keep praying for him.

Thursday, July 21, 2005

We saw Dr. Case today. It's still just a waiting game. He also mentioned that he wants Nick to see an infectious disease doctor before the next surgery so he can figure out antibiotic coverage. Nick has been on an antibiotic, or two, for every surgery. He is concerned that Nick might develop a resistance to antibiotics if he doesn't switch what is prescribed.

After Dr. Case, Nick and I went to my office to take intraoral photos of his mouth. The skin graft that Dr. Case took from his thigh, and placed under his tongue, is still growing hair. Hair in his mouth! It looks nasty! I could see the follicles on the screen. The hair follicles should eventually die off, but what a surprise that was for us. It was a gross surprise. The human body is just bizarre.

Saturday, July 23, 2005

When people have commented how strong I am, all I can think is, my husband is strong. I'm just part of his support team. I cry. It's usually when I'm alone and not in front of anyone, but I cry. I'm afraid. Every single day, I am afraid. But today, I met a new low.

We went to a civil war reenactment today. We were walking around, checking out the tents and the craftsmen, when the black powder guns went off. I just about lost it. It took everything in me not to burst into tears. All I could think of was, that type of gun ruined my husband's life. That's what he heard after he got shot. I felt crazy to be reacting that way, but I simply couldn't help the affect it had on me. I could see him in my mind's eye, spinning around with the impact. Falling backward. Gurgling into the walkie talking. Tucking his chin and walking to get help. I felt like I was losing my mind even thinking about it.

Monday, July 25, 2005

    I had an eye doctor appointment today. I was nervous to go because Cary and my relationship has been very strained since Brandon's court date. I assumed it was because of my letter.

    Apparently, Brandon never let Cary read the letter I wrote. She said that his actions, though, led her to believe that our friendship was over. I told her the contents of the letter. I told her that I'm afraid that Brandon will hesitate to defend himself and she would end up in the same predicament that I am in or worse. She and I hugged and cried together. I refuse to lose my best friend over this stupid accident. She and I need each other!

    This afternoon, Nick took Kenzie and I to the farm where he was shot. He wanted to see the farmer and thank him for his help that night. The farmer and his family are wonderful people. I was glad to meet them. They sincerely care about us. Kenzie also enjoyed meeting all their animals!

Friday, July 29, 2005

We grabbed a chance to camp with my parents this weekend. Kenzie and I spent the day today swimming with Krista and Gwen. It was fun watching the girls play. Mom and Dad are keeping Gwen overnight tonight so that Krista and John can go out for dinner.

We all ate supper together, and while I was cleaning up dishes with Mom, Nick was dancing with Kenzie. Suddenly, Kenzie started crying and holding her elbow. She wouldn't let go of it, nor would she move it.

Nick and I decided to take her to the Emergency Room when she still couldn't move it or hold her sippy cup after ten minutes. She kept crying and saying, "Mommy, me me belbow hurts!"

We waited five hours in the Emergency Room with Kenzie softly sobbing on my lap. They finally brought us in and the physician diagnosed Nursemaid's Elbow. It literally took the doctor about five seconds to pop it back into place. The doctor was very upset with the triage nurse for not getting Kenzie in right away because it was such an easy fix instead of making a child hurt for five hours.

On the way back to the campground, Kenzie was her perky self. She kept informing us of the traffic lights, "Daddy…Green light…go!" I love that cute little voice and hated hearing her cry tonight. This was our family's fifth trip to the Emergency Room in seven months. It's getting ridiculous!

Saturday, July 30, 2005

Krista and John came to the campground early and made French toast for everyone. The kids played at the playground and swam in the pond.

Cary and her daughter came to visit. Kenzie held little Elizabeth and loved it! They brought sand and garden toys for Kenzie as a belated birthday gift.

Cary and I had a long talk alone too. The accident has been so hard on us and our friendship. Brandon has distanced himself from us and that makes Cary uncomfortable. I let her know that he has nothing to do with our friendship and she shouldn't feel bad.

I have such a hard time when she keeps telling me to "Give it up to God". I am a good Catholic, but hearing it repeatedly gets old. I finally shared my feelings with her. She was very understanding, and I honestly feel that she is at a loss for words sometimes because she feels so bad. I am so thankful that we can talk about anything.

Monday, August 8, 2005

Nick went to see Brandon yesterday after speech therapy. Brandon was working on building his and Cary's new home. Nick asked Brandon to tell him what happened on the day of the accident. Brandon just clammed up and didn't say a word. I could understand when Brandon couldn't say anything before, but since he's had his day in court, I truly feel that he owes Nick an explanation now. If it is too hard for Brandon to talk about, I completely understand that, but at least tell Nick that.

When I did Nick's wound care yesterday, I noticed a new area that was bleeding under the right side of his jaw, so I called Dr. Case for an appointment.

Dr. Case saw Nick today and he feels that there is no significant change or reason for concern. He will see Nick again on September 1st.

Today, I noticed a bump directly above Nick's feeding tube. The last time this happened, they said it was a pulled muscle. We will have to watch it.

Wednesday, August 17, 2005

We headed out this morning in our camper, towing my car. My parents followed in their camper with Krista, John, and Gwen. We were heading north for a five-day weekend at Fairieland and Bear Country.

We got about twenty minutes from home when our camper started to shake and shimmy like crazy. Three minutes later we heard a loud thump, so Nick pulled off the exit. We had lost the treads off one of our rear, dual tires. Nick and John unhooked my car and drove forty minutes to get two new tires then bring them to a local garage to be mounted before coming back to us.

We finally made it to our campground around 4:30pm. We had to repair a couple of closet poles from the bumping around when the tire blew, but thankfully we got here safely.

We will still have to deal with Nick's care and feeding tube, but at least we are escaping for a bit. I am so excited to see the kids ride the rides and play!

Wednesday, August 24, 2005

Nick's feeding tube stoma is leaking. Thank God this didn't happen when we were on our camping trip!

Nick visited the trauma surgeon today and had to have a new tube placed. Apparently, the balloon that held the old one in place had leaked its water out, so the tube was ready to fall out when Nick got there. Nick feels much better now.

Brandon called today. It's been three weeks since Nick visited him. He still barely spoke. I tend to wonder why he calls. He doesn't speak, nor does he ask Nick any questions. Is it a sense of duty?

Monday, August 29, 2005

    Last Thursday, when I did Nick's care, I noticed that his chin bone looked like it was starting to protrude. It really freaked me out, so I called Dr. Case's office. I was told, "Don't focus on it, it will be fine". Needless to say, I WAS focusing on it, so Nick recommended that we take Kenzie to our local country fair. Watching her dance in the bleachers at the concert there helped. We saw quite a few people that we know, and Kenzie loved touring the animal barns. Nick made a good call getting me to go.
    This morning, I have no doubt that the bone is getting ready to fall out, yet Dr. Case feels there is no reason to see Nick. I am so worked up; my stomach is killing me. I just feel like we're completely alone in deciphering how bad things look. How can Dr. Case hear that his patient's bone is looking like it will fall out and not want to see it for himself?

Thursday, September 1, 2005

    A large piece of Nick's chin bone came out last night. I could have vomited. I took photos of Nick's chin wound and of the piece of bone that came out next to a ruler. The piece is an inch long by three quarters of an inch wide. I've been taking photographs all along in the hope that being able to show doctors the stages he is going through, will help with plans for reconstruction of his jaw.
    We went to see Dr. Case this morning. He okayed a new swallow evaluation. He said he wants to do a brachial artery surgery, which would take tissue and blood supply from Nick's arm, to cover the existing reconstruction plate.
    Dr. Case said that he had spoken to Dr. Bennett about Nick also. Dr. Bennett feels that the current reconstruction plate should be removed as well as any bone fragments. He would then place a new plate and cover it with the brachial artery.
    We made an appointment for October 17th at 5am to meet with both doctors at Dr. Bennett's office. This way they can discuss the options while looking at Nick together. I just pray they make the right decision. Once again, they are talking about taking another healthy piece of Nick and moving it. As far as I can tell, the pectoral muscle surgery was not as successful as they hoped.

Friday, September 2, 2005

    Nick and I went to his swallow study today. He was able to eat applesauce, pudding, and soggy cheerios. It took him about ten minutes to eat four cheerios, but at least he could eat them.

    We were a bit let down by how difficult it was for him to manipulate the food since he can't use his tongue, but we were thrilled he could eat at all.

    Unfortunately, now he's on hold again. His chin started leaking tonight. We're both disgusted. I feel so bad for Nick. Every time he takes one step forward, he takes two steps back. He's back to using only the feeding tube.

Wednesday, September 6, 2005

    The leaking from Nick's chin has been getting progressively worse every day. I called Dr. Case's office yesterday, but he never called back with a recommendation.

    Wanda from Dr. Case's finally called back today and told us that Dr. Case wants Nick to stop speech and swallow therapy for now due to the leak. He is not to put anything in his mouth. No kidding! It's not like we've been through this before. Of course, he stopped eating by mouth. But what now?

    Nick and I are both cranky and disgusted. I feel like we're living retirement life way too early. You know, the time when you're both home together, day in and day out. One spouse is sickly, and the other takes care of them. This isn't supposed to happen in your thirties! Nick hasn't worked since December, and he is absolutely stir crazy. We are driving each other nuts!

Thursday, September 15, 2005

Nick, Kenzie, Gwen, and I had a fun day playing inside. We made a "tent city" out of chairs and blankets then had lunch in there. We gave the girls blanket "swing" rides and read to them. We really enjoyed them!

Nick also lost another piece of bone from his chin. Thankfully, keeping busy with the kids kept our minds off our anxiety.

Brandon, Cary, and Elizabeth came over for pizza tonight. Nick had already had his tube feeding before they got here. Since Nick couldn't eat, Brandon refused to eat too. It made Nick and I very uncomfortable knowing that Brandon was probably hungry but wouldn't eat in front of Nick. It was ridiculous.

Cary laid Elizabeth down on my bed, then she and I had a heart-to-heart talk. She told me that Brandon won't share his feelings with her at all. He refuses to talk about the accident with her and she feels that there is an emotional wall between them. I wish that Brandon would speak to someone. Keeping all his feelings to himself is not healthy in a situation like this.

Saturday, October 1, 2005

    Krista called this morning to ask us to go apple and pumpkin picking. The kids were adorable stumbling through the pumpkin patch and picking their favorite orange ball.

    When we got home, I planted two hundred flower bulbs and spread mulch. Just before I put supper on the table, Kenzie climbed up in her highchair on the side of me and said, "Mommy, you me me best friend." Oh, my goodness that child melts my heart!

    The three of us went to Krista, John, and Gwen's tonight. They were having a group of friends over for volleyball. Nick used to play but hasn't since the accident for fear of hurting his jaw worse. It was fun to see everyone and visit though!

Thursday, October 6, 2005

    Nick had an appointment with Dr. Case this morning. He said that Nick can have anything that he can drink through a straw. Though Nick is happy to be able to have food, I really wonder if it's a good idea since he is still leaking. I can't imagine that having food go into whatever crevices there are will allow for healing. But we will see.

    Tonight, I attempted to puree cheese raviolis for Nick. Note to self, don't EVER try that again! It was WAY too thick and VERY gross! It made a nasty paste that I had a hard time cleaning out of the blender, never mind trying to suck it through a straw.

Monday, October 10, 2005

    Nick seems to be much happier lately. I think it's the food. Since he got the OK to drink through a straw last week, he has had pureed food every day. He had pureed burgers on Friday night, a puree of pot roast, broccoli and winter squash on Saturday night, and pureed chicken with mashed potatoes and carrots on Sunday.
    To the girl who always separated her food on her plate when she was growing up, the thought of pureeing everything together has the distinct feel of pre-chewed food to me. That just goes to show you, we don't appreciate what we have, until we don't have it.

Monday, October 17, 2005

Kenzie had a sleepover at my parent's house last night so Nick and I could leave our house by 3:45 am for the much waited for appointment with Dr. Case and Dr. Bennett. It was over an hour drive to Dr. Bennett's main office.

Dr. Case had wanted this consultation because he, being a plastic surgeon, he deals primarily with tissue. Dr. Bennett, being an oral maxillofacial surgeon, deals primarily with bone, so the two together should have been able to decide on a plan to reconstruct Nick. I say "should have" because Dr. Case never showed up.

Dr. Bennett tried calling Dr. Case, but he didn't pick up, so Dr. Bennett evaluated Nick and told him his thoughts. He said that he would speak with Dr. Case then call us to further discuss the options. I can't believe that Dr. Case blew off another doctor, never mind us! That is so unprofessional!

Thursday, October 20, 2005

Dr. Bennett finally heard from Dr. Case and called us. He said that he and Dr. Case do not agree on the next step. Dr. Case wants a CT scan next, and Dr. Bennett feels that Dr. Case is procrastinating because Dr. Case told him that every time he treats Nick, he "gets burned".

If Dr. Case feels that way, and honestly, it's true, why the heck didn't he pull up his big boy pants and admit he needed help months ago? Some doctors have such a God complex! A truly good doctor can admit when they are out of their comfort zone and refer to someone who specializes. It's no different than what I have seen in dentistry over the years.

Why do some of these doctors use their patients as guinea pigs then discard them when they can't figure out how to fix them? I can't help but think of the time Dr. Case wasted just waiting for Nick to heal.

After talking with Dr. Bennett, we agreed to meet with him and Dr. Case's senior partner, Dr. Carter. Dr. Bennett will call us once he speaks with Dr. Carter.

Tuesday, November 1, 2005

As of October 26th, Nick told Dr. Bennett that he wanted him and Dr. Carter to take over. We are just waiting to get them together now.

I wrote a letter to request all of Nick's records from Dr. Case for Dr. Bennett. We need to do it officially even though Dr. Case abandoned Nick.

Nick wants to send his letter to Harris hospital and the state Department of Health about the nursing abuse that he suffered in the hospital. I know it weighs on his mind, but I hope I can get him to hold off a bit longer until he is done with surgeries.

Brandon came over to visit Nick today. The visits are further and further apart now and still mostly silent on Brandon's part.

We are excited that Gloria will be flying in for a visit on Thursday! We have really missed her, and I know she is dying to see Nick.

Friday, November 18, 2005

    The last couple of weeks have been a blur. Nick had a CT scan with dye and insisted on my help to finish his letter to the state and hospital. It was against my wishes, but he sent it off last Friday. I have been praying that he doesn't end up regretting it the next time he has surgery.

    Having Gloria here has been nice but no one, including Nick, can seem to make any decisions without me. They can't even decide what type of snack is okay for Kenzie! Nick is becoming totally reliant on me for things he has always done for himself.

    I'm not feeling well again, and it seems that the little things just stress me out so easily right now. I know I am irritable, and I hate it.

    Today, I received a phone call from the head nurse at Harris hospital. She said that they had received Nick's complaint letter and she was horrified. She will investigate and wanted to let us know that neither nurse is still employed by the hospital. In fact, one has left the state. If nothing else, that gives us less to worry about for the next surgery.

Sunday, November 20, 2005

Kyle and Brandon came over yesterday to ask Nick to pull a ticket for a raffle drawing on a weathervane. They had organized yet another fundraiser. I can't believe how many people are still doing such kind things to support us! Before they left, the guys gave us a hefty donation from the raffle. God is so good to us!

When Kenzie woke up from her nap yesterday, my parents joined us at the Riverwalk for dinner to celebrate Gloria's birthday. I had called ahead in the morning to be sure that we could blend Nick's meal and they had agreed to it. Our waitress, Karen, was wonderful about taking Nick's filled blender into the kitchen to blend his meal for him. That was our very first meal at a restaurant together since the accident and it was a success!

John had been given tickets to a professional football game for today and he offered them to us. I spent a bit of time this week trying to get approval for Nick to take his pureed food in to the stadium with us, but we have everything in writing and today was the day!
We had fabulous seats and our team won! We had a marvelous time, and it was awesome to have a date! What a great weekend!

Thursday, November 24, 2005, ~ Thanksgiving Day

    It snowed last night so Nick and Kenzie had fun outside while Gloria and I prepared dinner. Nick ran up and down the driveway pulling her in her sled while she giggled.

    Gloria and I had quite a laugh too. I had asked her to peel potatoes while I was in the shower. When I came downstairs, I found that she had peeled the entire ten-pound bag! There are only going to be six of us at dinner. We will be swimming in mashed potatoes around here for a week! It cracked me up because she raised five children, so she should know how many potatoes it takes to feed just six people. Yes, the teasing was a lot of fun, and thankfully Gloria is a good sport.

    My parents joined us for dinner, and we all took part in our tradition of writing what we are thankful for on the tablecloth with permanent marker. I truly enjoy this tradition because it gives me the feeling that my aunts, uncles and grandparents are still with us at the table.

    After dinner, Nick took a bunch of food to his coworkers at the jail and thanked them for everything that they have done for us. They may be working, but they got a taste of a Thanksgiving dinner!

Friday, November 25, 2005

    Nick and I went to see Dr. Bennett today for a recheck. He ended up removing four screws from the front portion of Nick's chin. They were no longer holding the bone segment in place since that segment came out in pieces for me over the last month when I have been doing his care. Nick will be better off without them.

    He told Nick and I that he is not planning any surgeries for Nick until January, but next week we will meet with him and Dr. Carter to discuss the next steps. I'm happy that we will have a consultation with the two of them, but January feels so far away.

Sunday, November 27, 2005

A local town has a light parade every year on the Sunday after Thanksgiving. We went tonight with my parents, Gloria, Krista, John, and Gwen. It was freezing cold with some snow flurries too, but the lights were beautiful.

I had packed thermoses filled with creamy, hot chocolate for all of us and snacks for the kids too. Their little eyes lit up when they saw dancing reindeer and, of course, Santa Claus.

There were high school marching bands, and choirs playing and singing traditional holiday tunes. Horses had festively decorated manes, and the antique cars, and firetrucks were adorned with lights. Several beautiful floats commemorated the birth of Christ, while others held gingerbread houses and winter wonderlands.

Gloria had never seen anything like it before. She kept saying, "Oh wow" as each new float turned the corner in our direction. We really enjoyed sharing our tradition with her. What a great night!

Friday, December 2, 2005

Kenzie hasn't been sleeping well this week. She was cranky all day yesterday because Gloria flew home. That little girl loves playing with her grandmother and the feeling is quite mutual. The two of them are great at playing make believe games together. Kenzie's favorite make-believe game is "animal". Either she, or we, pretend we're a pet or wild animal and crawl around on the floor.

Today, Kenzie and Gwen played, and Krista and I chatted. Lately, Kenzie has been getting very tired and having an emotional breakdown every morning around 11:30. Well, as 11:30 approached, and she got crankier by the minute, Krista said, "Five more minutes until meltdown."

We could not help but laugh when Kenzie stopped dead in her tracks and said, "What?!?! Me, me gonna melt?!?" The kid had such a shocked and scared look on her face when she said it too. I guess there has been a little bit too much of *Frosty the Snowman* watching in this house this week!

Wednesday, December 7, 2005

I woke up a lot from anxiety attacks last night, so I was exhausted all day.

Nick went to the jail again today. He wants to be sure that he thanks all three shifts in some way. He brought coffee and doughnuts for the first shift workers and said thank you to them during roll call.

We met with our lawyer this morning to revise our wills to add Kenzie. We never gave it as much thought as we have since the accident. We want to be sure that if something were to happen to us, that she is well cared for and financially provided for as well.

Brandon, Cary, and Elizabeth came to visit for two hours tonight. Brandon goes back in uniform tomorrow. I am so disgusted with the state. Aren't they worried that he'll misjudge while in uniform?

Nick lost two more pieces of bone from his chin today. I can't believe he still has bone left to lose. It seems that I have been finding more that came to the surface for weeks.

Saturday, December 10, 2005

The three of us were eating breakfast this morning when Nick said, "I think we have a problem." His pureed eggs were coming out of his stomach near the feeding tube hole and there was a puddle on the floor.

I called his trauma surgeon and he recommended that we go to the Emergency Room at Harris Hospital. We dropped Kenzie at Krista's and headed out.

They checked his feeding tube and did an x-ray. The physician removed only 2cc of water from the feeding tube balloon. That's way too little. The balloon had leaked out 8cc of water. He added 10cc in and three hours later, we were allowed to leave.

Never a dull moment around here.

Tuesday, December 13, 2005

  Nick and I went to Dr. Bennett's for the consultation appointment with him and Dr. Carter. Our first impression of Dr. Carter was great!
  He and Dr. Bennett looked Nick over and discussed where they would make incisions. They told us that Dr. Bennett would extract Nick's lower left canine tooth and remove loose bone under anesthesia in the office.
  The next surgery would include removing the reconstruction plate and replacing it. They would move the neck tissue up to cover his chin and advance Nick's tongue and floor of the mouth (the pectoral muscle) forward and into the proper position. They may need to make a relief cut in the pectoral muscle to move it. They may also need a skin graft on his neck.
  They told us that the pectoral muscle can never be put back into Nick's chest, but once it grows blood supply, a portion of it that runs through his neck can be removed. The skin graft could then be removed, and his neck skin rejoined.
  The two doctors joked with us very comfortably and picked on each other too. Dr. Bennett laughed and told us that Dr. Case told him that he might get a bone scan on Nick. He left us high and dry, and he is acting like he's still Nick's surgeon? He is so pompous. Does he not realize that we're done with him or is he just afraid to admit it to Dr. Bennett?

Tuesday, December 20, 2005

    I had a horrendous night last night. I had major anxiety attacks and Kenzie woke up at 3:30am and vomited everywhere. Shortly after, I vomited too.

    I have no doubt that the anxiety has a lot to do with the fact that today is the one-year anniversary of the accident. I can't help but relive that night in my head. I know that Nick has been thinking about it a lot too.

    I made an appointment with my physician to discuss the anxiety. I am losing too much sleep because of it.

    Nick has more loose bone in his jaw. I just pray that eventually he will heal and have a somewhat normal life.

Sunday, December 25, 2005, ~ Christmas Day

After a week of anxiety attacks, one of which was on the verge of being debilitating in Walmart because I felt like I couldn't move, we finally made it to Christmas.

Kenzie left out her toy, plastic milk, and cookies as well as homemade cookies for Santa last night but had totally forgotten that it was Christmas when she woke up this morning. Once she remembered, she was so excited to get down the stairs we couldn't move fast enough.

When she got to the kitchen, she was very upset to see that Santa had not only eaten the cookies, but also took her play milk and cookies. I checked her toy grocery cart and showed her that Santa had put her toys away. He must have been trying to help her clean up. Kenzie loved the gifts that Santa brought and like most kids her age, the boxes were a big hit too!

Krista made a spiral ham, and we had an excellent visit with my parents, Krista, John, and Gwen. The girls played with Gwen's gifts from Santa as well as a couple of toys that Kenzie brought over to show Gwen too.

The only downfall to the day was the bone chip in Nick's chin that was throbbing like a toothache. I felt so bad for him. He's really hurting.

Wednesday, December 28, 2005

  This morning, Nick removed the loose bone from his chin himself. It was about three-quarters of an inch long and it had visible lines from the screws that had been drilled into it. I photographed it next to a ruler like I have with the other pieces. We are constructing what is turning out to be a very gory photo album as Nick goes through the steps of being put back together.
  Nick took me to my Upper G.I. series appointment to see what is going on with the massive reflux that I am having. Then, we went to Dr. Bennett's office for Nick's appointment. Dr. Bennett just cleaned out the area where the bone came out and placed two sutures.
  Tonight, we're both very upset. Nick has A LOT of saliva dripping out of his chin again. We called Dr. Bennett and he told Nick to use the feeding tube and nothing by mouth for now. We are both very discouraged. Life is nothing but a rollercoaster ride of emotions. I know everyone deals with these rollercoasters, but the last year has had more lows than highs for our family.

Thursday, December 29, 2005

My physician called an antibiotic in to my pharmacy for me. My white blood cells are over eleven and they should be below five. I have an infection somewhere in my body but she's not sure where. At least I know I'm not losing my mind when I feel lousy.

Nick called Brandon to cancel our New Year's Eve plans with him, Cary, and Elizabeth. We are so disgusted with Nick's lack of healing that we just don't feel like seeing Brandon. I feel bad because I would like to spend time with Cary, but right now, we just can't.

The hole in Nick's chin is now the size of a dime with even more saliva flowing from it. It feels like we're starting from square one again. One of his sutures had already pulled through the tissue so I removed it tonight. I'm so upset with this situation; I could have cried all day.

Friday, December 30, 2005

    Under the recommendation of my physician, I went to see a counselor today. She listened to me as I relayed my anxieties and fears. She told me that what I am feeling is normal for all the trauma that our family has been through. Normal…what a funny thought. She prescribed an antianxiety medication to help me through all of this.

    I find that I keep questioning how this accident could have happened. Why does Brandon still refuse to talk to Nick about it? His trial is over, and he should know by now that Nick would never press charges. He owes Nick an explanation.

    Tonight, I got mad at Nick because he kept saying, "Fuck!" or "Mother fucker!" or "Fucking (insert word)", in front of Kenzie. Of course, he's hard to understand and she doesn't seem to be catching what he's saying, but there's no excuse for it. I know he's disgusted because of the saliva pouring out of his chin, but our two-year-old doesn't need to hear that language.

    I called Dr. Bennett about the sutures coming out and the abundance of saliva. He never called me back. Life is just one frustration after another. I just don't see a light at the end of this tunnel.

Saturday, December 31, 2005, ~ New Year's Eve

Krista, John, Gwen, and my parents came for pizza and to watch movies tonight. My parents stayed to play cards after my sister and her family went home and I put Kenzie to bed. It was a nice, quiet, New Year's Eve.

Nick surprised me with a back massage tonight. It was the most relaxed that I have been in a while and having him close to me and touching me was wonderful. I miss our closeness. I find that I am in mourning of it now. Knowing that our intimacy will never be the same breaks my heart.

The hole under his chin keeps getting bigger and bigger. The poor man is so disgusted, and I don't blame him one bit. I pray to God that he heals. Hopefully 2006 will be a better year.

Monday, January 2, 2006

    I have felt like an elephant is sitting on my chest all day. I feel like I can't take a deep breath. I'm wondering if it's indigestion from the antibiotic that I'm on or maybe the new anxiety medication. How funny would it be if the anxiety medication GAVE me anxiety?

    Nick's sister Melanie is pushing us to let her write to Oprah Winfrey about the accident to see if Oprah can help get other doctors for Nick. We know that Melanie's heart is in the right place, but the last thing we want right now is an invasion of privacy like that.

    Dr. Bennett finally returned my call from the other day. He recommended that we schedule an appointment with him for next week. Nick told him that we can now see a screw and a plate inside the hole. I wish he would have told Nick to schedule something for THIS week!

Thursday January 5, 2005

    I went to my therapist, Mary Anne, today. She gave me a copy of a "Personal Bill of Rights". There are so many things on it that I have not allowed for myself. The biggest one is, "I have a right to say no to requests or demands that I can't meet." I am so busy trying to make everyone else comfortable and happy, I don't even think to say, "No, I've done enough." The reality is that I feel I should help whenever possible. Nick needs me and so does Kenzie. Everyone around us has been so generous and caring. I feel a strong need to repay them in any small way that I can.
    I am also struggling to separate myself from feeling that I am going through the trauma. When Nick's jaw gets worse, I feel like my world will end. Though he IS my world, my own personal world will not end with the backslides. In order for me to have the strength to deal with everything and support him, I need to remember that and control my anxiety. I have not told Mary Anne that I feel that way yet. I feel selfish for feeling it.
    Nick, Kenzie, and I went to visit my parents and they had some of their friends there too. It was nice to just sit and laugh with them. I think that I may tell Cary that I can't see Brandon for a while. It's just not good for me. He doesn't talk and he mopes so much. And to be honest, I'm angry that he won't tell Nick what happened.

Friday, January 6, 2006

Oh, my goodness I had fun with Kenzie today! She and Nick came to my office, and I cleaned her teeth for the first time. She was so adorable!

After I finished her teeth, she wanted to clean mine. I put her in a mask and gloves with my safety glasses and I laid in the chair. I gave her a mouth mirror and the suction to use. That child just giggled and giggled as she suctioned my tongue and it made funny noises. Her laugh was contagious and the three of us ended the visit with a group hug. Nick took some great pictures to remember this fun afternoon.

Tonight, our friend Dean came over with his son Collin. The two kids had a lot of fun playing in the playroom.

After a little while, Kenzie came to alert me that Collin was going on the big boy toilet and he "pees out his belly button." While I should have told her that it's not nice to follow someone into the bathroom, it honestly took everything in me not to pee my pants laughing, and I just let it slide. Kids are hilarious!

Wednesday, January 11, 2006

My Dad came over at 6:30am to stay with Kenzie until she woke up. Nick and I went for bloodwork then went to Dr. Bennett's office for 8:15.

He said that the tissue looks better but he has no surgery date set yet. He said that the latest that the surgery would be scheduled is the beginning of March. We are so upset. This just keeps dragging on and on. Nick wants to eat!

I went to work after Nick's appointment then came home to a very excited Kenzie. She kept hugging and kissing me, and I relished every second.

Nick let me know that Cary had called for me while I was at work. I returned her call only to cringe when Brandon stiffly answered the phone. It is so uncomfortable to talk to him. He has no interest in talking to me either so thankfully he handed the phone over to Cary quickly.

I thought that I would get a chance for a shower alone tonight. Last night, I told Nick that ten minutes alone in the bathroom would be like gold to me. I gave Kenzie a bath in her bathroom, then handed her off to Nick to get her dressed. I went in our bathroom to shower, and he brought Kenzie in there to get her dressed. I feel like I talk to myself sometimes because he is definitely not hearing my requests. Why bring her in our bathroom at all? I just wanted ten minutes of peace.

Tuesday, January 17, 2006

Dr. Bennett's office called to inform us that Nick's surgery is scheduled for January 23rd. They want Nick at their office for 9am tomorrow and we need to schedule him for a full pre-op physical by this Friday. We were shocked and happy to hear that he didn't have to wait until March!

I called Nick's new physician's office and was told that they need one month's notice for a physical. I explained that we just found out about the surgery today. They wouldn't ask the doctor if they could schedule it, so I called her husband, Kenzie's pediatrician, to ask for his help.

A little while later, we received a call from the doctor's office. They gave Nick an appointment for 3:45 tomorrow afternoon but won't guarantee that the paperwork will be done in time. I understand that this is a last-minute request on our part, but for goodness sake, they know what Nick is going through! He has been seen there several times already.

I called my office to cancel my patients for tomorrow morning. I want to be with Nick to hear what Dr. Bennett has planned for this surgery. I also called my mom and Gloria to let them know that there is a change in plans.

In the midst of all this chaos, Brandon called and asked if he could visit at either 4:30 or 7:30pm today. Nick told him that either time would be fine. Well, Brandon never showed up, nor did he call to say that his plans had changed. The anxiety that I was feeling over having to see him was for absolutely nothing. Unfortunately, that just gave me one more reason to be irritated with him.

Wednesday, January 18, 2006

Nick and I spent two hours with Dr. Bennett this morning. He explained everything and even wrote out the prescriptions that Nick will need once he is discharged so that I can have them filled and waiting for him when he gets home from the hospital.

The lack of prescription planning with Dr. Case had always been extremely stressful in the past. I have usually had to run around trying to find liquid medications for Nick's feeding tube. The liquid form of the medications is not usually carried by pharmacies, so I have often had to drive forty-five minutes in one direction just to get one prescription. Dr. Bennett's planning ahead is wonderful!

I worked this afternoon and came home to a house without electricity. Nick had just gotten home from his physical. His doctor did not give him the completed paperwork but promised that she would fill it out tonight. She apologized for her staff as well.

He and I packed our clothes, suction, medications, etc., and came to my parents. They have electricity so the three of us will stay here until ours comes back on. Our neighbor, Eloise, let me know that the windstorm that we're having toppled a tree onto the power lines at her end of the road. The tree is on fire so it may be a while.

It feels so strange to be sleeping at my parents. We're in twin beds with Kenzie in a crib between us. Thank God we have a nice warm place to stay!

Sunday, January 22, 2006

After four and a half days, we have electricity!! Nick and I have been running back and forth between my parents' house and ours to run our generator so that the water pipes don't freeze and take care of the dogs. Thank goodness my parents only live a mile away!

I've been a nervous wreck that we might miss the hospital's pre-op phone call while we were at my parents' house too. I called the hospital to give them my parents' number as well. Thankfully, we got the call this afternoon when we got home.

Nick has also been dealing with a faulty Automatic Braking System light on his truck. The dealership has "fixed" it three times this week at a cost of over seven hundred dollars, and it's still on.

Cary called today to wish Nick "Good luck" for his surgery tomorrow and she told him that she will keep him in her prayers. We have not heard a word from Brandon since he never showed up for his visit.

Nick's left jaw is really bothering him. Dr. Bennett called tonight to check on Nick. We're very nervous about tomorrow, and of course, we're supposed to be getting snow too.

Monday, January 23, 2006

Nick and I were up by 3am and my parents were here by 3:50 so Mom could stay with Kenzie and Dad could come to Harris Hospital with us. It snowed the whole way there, but we made it!

Both Dr. Bennett and Dr. Carter came to speak with us prior to surgery. Dad and I sat in the Family Lounge from 7:30 am until 1pm.

Dr. Bennett came up to the lounge and told us that things went well. They lifted and moved the pectoral muscle forward and extracted Nick's remaining lower front teeth. They removed the "X" plate that we could see through the hole in his chin. They also removed the old reconstruction plate and placed a new plate. They were able to use existent tissue so there was no need for the radial forearm graft! Thank God!

My dad and I were finally able to see Nick at 4pm. He looked great considering the hell he had just been through. He has a drain sticking out of his neck for the pectoral muscle, and a bandage on his jaw but he is doing well.

Dad and I came home around 6:30pm. My mom is spending the night here with Kenzie and me.

Tuesday, January 24, 2006

Mom watched Kenzie today so Dad and I could go to visit Nick. When we got there, he was apparently feeling snarky because he had his sheets covering him and his johnny over his head when we walked in so we couldn't see how he looked. Unfortunately, right after that, he got nauseous and started vomiting. I can't imagine how much that must have hurt after mouth surgery.

The nurses gave Nick anti-nausea medications and that helped. He is very swollen but otherwise looks good. His drain was removed from his neck and Dr. Bennett told him that he has less chance of infection if he's at home, so he discharged him at 9pm tonight.

Dad and I got Nick home by 10pm and I got him settled in. He's both happy to be home, and nervous that something will go wrong. It's only been thirty-six hours since major surgery.

Friday, January 27, 2006

It has been two days of stress. Nick is in a lot of pain, so his blood sugars are elevated. Though this is normal when there's pain, it's also counterproductive for healing. Nick spent a lot of time walking around in the house to try to get his numbers down.

His feeding tube stoma keeps leaking too. It leaked three times yesterday so that meant a lot of clean up. I have been afraid to take my anxiety medication at night because it makes me sleepy, and I wouldn't be able to drive if we needed to head to the Emergency Room.

Today was Nick's post-op appointment with Dr. Bennett. He is happy with the results and hopes to have Nick eating pureed foods in two to three weeks. If that happens, the feeding tube can come out in four weeks, then Nick could possibly go back to work for the first time since the accident in about five weeks.

The next surgery will take place in about six months. At that time, Dr. Bennett wants to place bone beside the reconstruction plate. Six months after that, he would place dental implants.

Nick and I felt a glimmer of hope that there might be an end in sight. In the meantime, I am to clean the incision with half-strength peroxide, four times a day.

After we left Dr. Bennett, we went to the Trauma Clinic at Harris Hospital. What a fiasco! When the physician's assistant, Frieda, tried to drain the balloon on the feeding tube, there was nothing in it. She didn't know what to do so she called the Trauma Surgeon in. They decided to replace the feeding tube because the balloon was broken.

They considered using a Foley catheter as a feeding tube! Can you believe it?!? The biggest hospital in the state and they didn't think they had a G-Tube feeding tube!

They finally located one and replaced the old one. This one is smaller than the old one, so stomach contents will leak out until the hole closes around it. Poor Nick can't catch a break.

Sunday, January 29, 2006

    My parents got Kenzie and I out of the house for a bit today. Something as simple as getting groceries and a trip to McDonald's for lunch can take my mind off our troubles and make my day better.

    Nick was so disgusted today between blood sugar issues and bathroom issues, it was nice to get away a bit. He was angry with me for mentioning these issues to Dr. Bennett and told me that I was blowing it out of proportion. When he is so ridiculously cranky over something, who wouldn't think it bothers him? Needless to say, he has decided that he will try not taking his pain medication in the hope that the bathroom issue gets better.

    While I was altering Nick's feeding tube pouches so that they hold the new feeding tube comfortably, I couldn't help but stew on the fact that it has been six days since his surgery, and we have not heard from Brandon nor Cary to ask how it went. Brandon usually doesn't check on Nick, but Cary always does. I am between feeling hurt and wondering if something is wrong at their house.

Thursday, February 2, 2006

More scabs are coming off the incision every day. Nick's feeding tube leaked all over the kitchen floor this morning, so the floor got an unexpected washing, and my ears heard an unexpected rant of cursing.

Nick and I dropped Kenzie at my parents' house and went to Dr. Bennett's. He told us that "We're not out of the woods." He left in all the stitches as well. Nick and I were upset and just plain bummed out.

Kenzie brightened our day when we picked her up. She and Gwen had been playing, as is usual on the three days a week that my sister and I work. Kenzie told us that "Sassy", (Gwen's nickname) loves her and wants to marry her and give her flowers. Her little eyes sparkled when she said, "Mommy, I'm so excited to tell Auntie Krista that I'm going to marry her kid!" Kids are so hilarious!

Tonight, when I did Nick's care, there was a bit of serosanguinous fluid leaking from his neck. I'm worried.

Friday, February 3, 2006

    The saga of the truck ABS light continues. Nick brought his truck back to the dealership for the fourth time to have it fixed. When he picked it up, the light came back on. Nick freaked and honestly, I don't blame him. This has been totally ridiculous.

    Nick's buddy, Dean, came over and the two of them took apart his brakes to check them. Dean is a mechanic and he felt that Nick needed new brakes when he looked. The dealership said he didn't. Wouldn't you think the dealership would want to make money and replace them? I think it's pure laziness on their part.

    Dean stayed until 11pm reading the police report on the accident and Nick's letter about the nursing abuse. He let Nick talk about his questions on how the accident could have happened in the first place. Like Nick said, a person should be able to run buck naked through the forest and not get shot because hunters are supposed to identify what they're aiming at before they pull the trigger. Nick was wearing a lot of blaze orange on a day when snow was on the ground. It makes no sense.

    Reading the reports, Dean was very surprised at how close Brandon had been when he shot Nick. More than anything, having someone to talk to who won't judge was nice for Nick. Dean's such a good friend to us.

Monday, February 6, 2006

On Saturday, Nick and I went to the truck dealership with the photos that he and Dean had taken when they pulled Nick's brakes apart. They asked us to go back today to talk to the service manager.

Nick brought the truck back today and talked to the manager. He had their mechanics check it out and told Nick that they would look for his old ABS cluster because it appears that he didn't need the $700 new one after all. Nick asked for a refund and the manager said that he would talk to the owner and call Nick tomorrow.

Kenzie and I had fun shopping for materials and making Valentine cards today. It was good to get out and then get creative!

Tuesday, February 7, 2006

    Dr. Bennett removed all of Nick's scabs and stitches today. He said there is still a small hole in the mouth but that he feels it will fill in over time.

    I called the Department of Health regarding Nick's letter to them about the nursing abuse. They told me that we will have a response from them within a month. I explained that our goal is to make sure that no one else suffers at the hands of these two nurses. We do not want to sue.

    I had a terrible night last night. I had a wicked burning sensation in my chest. I think it's esophageal reflux. I also felt like someone was sitting on my chest again and I do tonight too. It concerns me because I get out of breath sometimes when I climb stairs too.

Wednesday, February 8, 2006

    The owner of the truck dealership called today. They will only give a very limited partial refund. That is ridiculous considering that they never fixed the problem and installed something that wasn't needed! Nick started writing letters to the truck company, the Department of Motor Vehicles, and the Department of Consumer Protection. He feels victimized again, but this time he is strong enough to do something about it.
    I received a bill from Dr. Bennett's office for Nick's extractions. Our insurance didn't cover it for some reason so I will have yet another phone call to make tomorrow.
    We did have a bit of fun with Kenzie today when we took her to her first movie at a theater. She loved the movie and the popcorn!
    This heaviness in my chest just seems to get worse every day. I took my anxiety medication in the hope that it helps. I'm starting to worry that there's something wrong with my heart.

Saturday, February 11, 2006

    Kenzie woke up at 2am with a horrible head cold. I spent the day helping her blow her nose every ten minutes. She even asked to lay down for her nap early. She woke up an hour later crying so I spent the afternoon rocking her as she slept on and off. The poor little peanut is so full of snot. She's coughing so hard that she's gagging.

    Nick and my relationship is suffering right now. He's so angry all the time. He barks at everyone including our parents. I know he's frustrated with his speech, but it's not our fault. We all try to understand him, but his mom, especially, gets very nervous that she won't understand him, and he'll get mad at her. The angrier he gets, the more frazzled she becomes and the harder it becomes for her to understand him. He's just never happy anymore.

Sunday, February 12, 2006

Dr. Bennett called today to check on Nick. When I told him that I'm working on the last few scabs, he yelled at me and said, "I removed the scabs! There shouldn't be any scabs!"

That did it. He pushed me over the edge. I responded to his yelling by saying, "If you didn't make him bleed like a stuffed pig when you removed the scabs, there wouldn't be any new ones for me to work on!"

I don't think he knew what to say. I would have never spoken to another professional that way, but his cocky surgeon attitude struck a chord with me today. I spend a lot of time taking care of Nick every day. Until he is here, seeing what I am seeing, Dr. Bennett needs to back off on his accusations.

I spent an hour and a half tonight soaking Nick's last two scabs with half strength peroxide on a cotton tipped applicator in an effort to remove them. I found a suture that looks like the type he has inside his mouth under the scab on the outside of his chin. With everything falling apart as often as it has, I can't help but wonder where this suture was initially.

Monday, February 13, 2006

Nick brought the truck back to the dealership again and did nothing but complain about his experience when he got home. Kenzie was whining and needy because of her cold, and I tried to clean the house while I made every effort to ignore a romping headache.

I am so absolutely disgusted with Nick. He hasn't been helping with Kenzie at mealtime because he doesn't sit with us. He pushes his syringes of food into his feeding tube then leaves to do something else. Our family mealtime is non-existent.

He forgets everything now too. He told me that he'd help me to clean today but he didn't. I tried to get ready for bed tonight, and instead of helping with Kenzie, he got on the phone. It's like he is living an entirely separate life. I finally had had it tonight. I told him, "I've taken care of you for the last fourteen months and you can't even give me ten minutes!"

I feel bad because I know he's just miserable. This is not what a young man's life should look like by any means. But we have to get through this together as a team if we're going to get through it at all. He doesn't seem to see what is going on here. I hate our life right now.

Tuesday, February 14, 2006

    Nick brought home fresh flowers for Kenzie and I for Valentine's Day. They were beautiful!
    We decided to bring Kenzie with us to Dr. Bennett's today, so we tried out our new portable DVD player in the back seat of the car. We stopped at Walmart, enroute to the doctor's office, and I ran in to grab a few groceries. I wasn't in there for ten minutes when Nick came in with Kenzie wrapped in his jacket. Apparently, watching the new DVD player made her car sick and she had vomited all over her winter coat and the back seat of my car. We didn't have enough time to go home before Dr. Bennett's, so we cleaned her up as much as possible and continued on. She vomited mucus once after that too. Colds and carsickness are not a good mix!
    Dr. Bennett said that things look good, and Nick can have pureed and soft foods now!! That's an awesome Valentine's gift!!

Wednesday, February 15, 2006

    Nick and Kenzie picked me up from work for a surprise lunch at McDonalds. Kenzie usually loves their indoor playscape, but today a little bully kept taunting her by yelling, "Baby in a diaper" and telling her that she was too little to play there. I reassured her, told her to ignore him, and to just enjoy playing. Some kids can be so mean.

    After work, I came home and made supper. I called Krista and Cary just to chat. Nick is now fixated on meeting with the Harris Hospital department heads, and I needed an ear or two to blow off steam. We all understand that he feels the need to make sure no one else is abused by those nurses, but until he is better, it's plain scary to pursue it.

    After I did Nick's incision care, he kept picking at a scab and uncovered another suture, one that should be inside his mouth. I could have cried. I pray that this last surgery doesn't fail. I'm also hurt that after I work on his care, he still feels the need to go over what I've done. He has always trusted me. He would never let his mom, the registered nurse, touch him, but he trusted me. I think he has too much time on his hands right now.

    I am so sick and tired of the constant upset in life. It's been fourteen months of worrying over one thing or another. It's no wonder that my stomach hurts!

Saturday, February 18, 2006

    Kenzie got very upset this morning because I came upstairs to get ready and left her with Nick. She started to come up the stairs by herself and Nick followed her. She kept yelling at him to stay downstairs. He got upset with her, picked her up, carried her upstairs kicking and screaming, and put her in her crib as a punishment. He angrily yanked the side of the crib up, and it came off in his hand. We ended up having to turn the crib into a daybed. Kenzie was thrilled. So much for her punishment.
    We mailed the complaint letters to the truck company, The Department of Motor Vehicles, and the Department of Consumer Protection today. It just seems that Nick is the one who gets victimized by Brandon, the nurses, or the truck dealership, and I'm the one doing all the paperwork and legwork!
    I was finally able to put Nick's suction machine away today. It will be so nice not to have to clean that thing daily! I also put away some of the medical supplies that we won't need anymore.
    Nick went out to a Ducks Unlimited dinner with his friend Don tonight. He had a great time and had no problem pureeing his meal. Kenzie was so excited about her "new" bed! She couldn't wait until naptime or bedtime. She absolutely loves her room now. It's crazy how we can screw up and it still works out for the best.

Monday, February 20, 2006

    I called Dr. Bennett today because I found areas that are bleeding and have pus on Nick's chin. He said that it's ok to return Nick's suction and make an appointment to have his feeding tube removed. I happily made both calls. I also called my physician about my nausea and reflux. She recommended that I double my stomach medication.
    This afternoon I had my annual gynecologist appointment. My blood pressure was 120/84. I told her that that is high for me. She told me to watch my diet and to exercise. The only problem is, I HAVE been watching my diet and exercising to help with my reflux and anxiety. I need to go back on March 6th for an ultrasound to check for polyps.
    I decided to check with my pharmacist about the medications that I am taking and my three recent experiences with elevated blood pressure. She told me that I'm taking 80mg over the recommended dose of my stomach medication and that that medication is known to cause high blood pressure. What the heck was my physician thinking to tell me to double the dose and not realize that it was the reason I was having the blood pressure issue? I decided to take myself off the medication and switch to an over-the-counter medication instead. I am also going to try using three pillows to elevate my head at night.
    Today was nurse Windy's last day with us. She has only been coming every three weeks now so we could order medical supplies, but it isn't necessary anymore. We are all going to miss her and her spunky personality.

Thursday, February 23, 2006

Nick and I went to see Dr. Bennett today. He said that it looks as though the hole in Nick's mouth is closing and everything else looks good. He also made a point of saying that Dr. Case didn't do anything wrong except postpone asking for help. He also blamed Dr. Case's postponement on a preoccupation due to his going through a divorce.

I hate to say it, but when you're a doctor, you shouldn't allow that to happen. I knew I couldn't work when the accident happened, so I took time off to focus on Nick. I realize not everyone is that lucky to be able to take time off for a hardship, but when people's lives are dependent on your clear thinking, you need to find a way to stay focused. Sometimes I wonder if the all-boy network comes in to play with doctors too. Dr. Bennett had no problem laughing at Dr. Case before. I wonder what happened to make him feel protective of him.

Nick told Dr. Bennett about the nurse abuse. He wasn't surprised.

I spoke to Cary today and Nick tried to see Brandon twice, but he wasn't home either time. Nick didn't call ahead because he feels that Brandon would just avoid him. He just wants to talk to him.

My blood pressure was 95/67 today! It pays to advocate for yourself. I still have a heavy feeling in my chest, but I'm feeling okay otherwise.

Saturday, February 25, 2006

Lisa, a Deputy Warden that works with Nick, came to visit today. Lisa is very savvy regarding investigations, internal affairs, and state laws. She came to review Nick's letters about the nursing abuse and gave us insight as to what to do. She is a very smart woman and very kind. She has offered to come to our meeting with the Harris Hospital department heads. We happily took her up on her offer.

Nick went to see Brandon. Brandon finally talked to Nick about the accident, though he didn't say much. He cried and said that it was an accident. He answered some, but not all, of Nick's questions.

I called Cary and admitted that I have been holding off on visiting with them because I was angry with Brandon for not answering Nick's questions until now. I told her that he finally talked to Nick today and now I hope our friendship with them as a couple, will be okay. She cried but thanked me for being honest and telling her everything because Brandon tells her nothing. What a lonely life that must be for her. Nick infuriates me sometimes, but at least we talk.

Monday, February 27, 2006

  I am still having a lot of chest discomfort that my doctor can't explain. She called and referred me to a Gastrointestinal Specialist for my reflux today.
  Nick and I went to Harris Hospital, and he had his feeding tube removed!! We are beyond thrilled! We also went to the floor in the hospital where we will be having our meeting with the department heads on Friday so we will know where to go.
  When we got home, my mom told me that she must repeat the right side of her mammogram. She is very worried. I am too. Hopefully it will be fine. One day at a time.
  The anxiety level is up. If nothing else, I can tell from the pain in my chest and stomach.

Friday, March 3, 2006

Nick had a swollen area in his mouth that looks like a mucocele, or blister. I called Dr. Bennett and he recommended that I pop it. I couldn't, so he told me to leave it alone.

Nick and I picked up Lisa and took her out to lunch before our meeting with the department heads at Harris Hospital. We discussed what we needed to focus on for the meeting.

The meeting was awful! I can't believe how little was documented. Nick's hospital records have no mention of the failed IV line with the swelling nor the scab on the top of his head. No one "remembers" that scab. It kills me that I had asked the trauma surgeon about the IV line AND the scab, he looked at both, and never documented either. Even nurse Rachel, the nurse we love and visit when we go up to the hospital, never documented the scab during her "intake review" when Nick was moved to her unit. She always seemed so on top of things. It is extremely frustrating! It all seems like a giant cover up and if I hadn't seen the swollen arm or bald spot on his head with a scab with my own two eyes, I wouldn't believe the abuse myself after reading the hospital records.

Nick and I brought Lisa home. She had asked questions on our behalf that were direct and to the point. She may not have been able to do much with the hospital board, but she won our admiration of her expertise.

When we picked up Kenzie, my mom could see the stress on my face, so she asked us to go out for dinner. Nick didn't feel like it, so Kenzie and I went without him.

Before today's meeting, I had gone through my diaries to write down the dates of the abuse and make notes about each occasion. I feel like it's fine for me to relive the hell of December 2004 repeatedly so that he can get some resolution, but he couldn't go out of his way for me to join us at dinner tonight. My feelings are hurt.

My stomach is in pain and my chest and shoulders are so tight, I could scream. I can't take this anymore. I am a complete and total mess.

Monday, March 6, 2006

    Nick went back to work for the first time today! He has been posted to the mail room while he continues to recover. I was so nervous and excited for him.

    The past fourteen months have felt like he retired too early due to health reasons, and I had to take care of him. Being together the six days a week that I am not at work leaves very little to talk about and too much to find fault with.

    I went to my ultrasound appointment today too. I don't have any cysts, polyps or fibroids causing my abdominal pain. While I am thrilled to find that out, I still have no idea what's making me hurt.

Tuesday, March 7, 2006

Kenzie and I rolled the coins that she had collected, then we went to the bank together. She handed the coin rolls to the teller and said, "Here's my pennies for college!" It was so cute.

Nick has had a couple of good days at work. They gave him a light duty post in the mailroom. I am thrilled that he won't have any inmate contact while he continues to heal. This job has him reviewing inmate mail with some awesome coworkers.

I chatted with Cary, then called our real estate attorney to ask him about a lawyer for the nursing abuse. He gave me the name of a malpractice attorney and I called. I only got three sentences out when he said, "I'm not interested in that type of case. Find someone else." I'm sure that since one of my sentences included, "we don't want to sue the hospital", our case quickly became a lot less interesting to him.

Dr. Bennett also called today to ask Nick to come to his house so he could take pictures of Nick for a presentation that he is doing. He knew that Nick had asked Dr. Case for photos from the Emergency Room on the night of the accident. Dr. Case had told Nick that no photos were taken because he's seen many cases like Nick's. Dr. Bennett told Nick that he knows those photos exist. If Nick makes the seventy-five-minute ride to his house to let him take photos of him now, he'll get him those photos and photos of all his surgeries. I hate feeling like Nick's being bribed, especially when he would have helped Dr. Bennett out anyway.

Thursday March 9, 2006

    I went to the G.I. specialist today. She gave me a new diet and new medications. I am to cut out tomatoes, tomato sauce, chocolate, fried foods, and anything mint plus multiple other foods. I hope it helps because those are some of my favorite foods.
    Nick and I went to Dr. Bennett's house for a 7:30pm meeting. He and his resident, who we fondly call "The Cookie Doctor" because he loved my Christmas cookies so much, took photos of Nick.
    The two doctors then showed us the photos of Nick right after the accident as well as the photos of the reconstructive surgeries, except for the pectoral muscle surgery. It was blatantly obvious that the reconstruction plate that Dr. Case had placed was about one inch larger than was necessary, and that's why it broke through Nick's thin jaw tissue. We could now see those plates side by side. The Cookie Doctor burned us a CD of the photos to take home.
    How could Dr. Bennett have said that everything Dr. Case did was fine? Maybe he hadn't seen those photos when he said it? Dr. Bennett also showed us photos of another reconstruction that he did. Before we left, he offered us the use of his property on a lake for fishing.
    Once we got home, I sat and read part of Nick's Harris Hospital records that came in the mail today. At our meeting with the department heads, they had agreed to mail us a free copy of Nick's records rather than charge us twenty-nine-cents a page for a two-hundred-fifty-page medical chart. Tomorrow I will print out the surgery photos, so I know we have a hard copy of those too.

Saturday, March 11, 2006

    Kenzie was very bratty today. I got so upset with her, I put her in her highchair for a time out. She then punched me in the right eye and knocked my contact out! I've never seen her like that before. Needless to say, she didn't get away with it and was punished by having to sit in her highchair facing the wall for ten minutes.

    Brandon, Cary, and Elizabeth came over to visit and have pizza tonight. Elizabeth nearly scared us to death when she choked on a play coin from Kenzie's cash register. Thank God Cary could reach in and get it out!

    I removed three sutures from Nick's chin tonight. He and I feel like we're finally getting closer and back on track with our marriage. I hate it when we argue or are just plain cranky with each other. We have both had our turns with that.

Tuesday, March 21, 2006

    Nick and Kenzie helped me to spring clean on Sunday. The teamwork was great!
    Sunday night, we went to the Civic Center with Krista, John, and Gwen to see *Monsters, Inc* on ice. Kenzie loved it!
    Krista was so careful to keep Kenzie and Gwen apart, especially in the car, because Kenzie has another cold. Well, on the way home, Gwen vomited. So much for keeping her healthy! Now I hope we don't catch what Gwen has.
    Nick has been having jaw pain on his right side since Sunday night. Today, after work, I met him at a commuter parking lot so we could go to Dr. Bennett's office.
    They did three kinds of x-rays to check the painful areas. Dr. Bennett said that the bone in the front of Nick's lower jaw looks "iffy". It had looked healthy when he did the surgery but now it's questionable. The segments of the bone have some play in them. He also feels that the pain is from clenching.
    He recommended that Nick have his remaining teeth fixed. Nick has a lot of chipped teeth, and one needs a root canal because it was so badly damaged in the accident. Once those are fixed, then Dr. Bennett would make Nick a nightguard. He gave Nick a prescription for Vicodin, and he also recommended Aleve.

Friday, March 24, 2006

    I spent the morning playing with Kenzie and Gwen. They love it when I serve them their snacks at the kiddie table with a towel draped over my arm. I use a French accent that keeps them giggling. I love making memories with those two!

    When Nick got home this afternoon, he and I brought Kenzie to my parents and headed to the Olive Garden for dinner. They seated us by the fireplace and were very nice about pureeing Nick's meal for him. We always carry one of his Magic Bullet blenders in the car, just in case, and tonight it came in very handy. Tonight, was the first time that he and I went out for a nice meal alone since Kenzie was born. I loved it!

    After dinner, we went to ToysRUs, Target, JCPenney, Sears, BabiesRUs, and Dicks to shop for Kenzie's Easter and birthday gifts. We did all of this and still made it home in time to put Kenzie to bed ourselves. What a great night!

Wednesday, March 29, 2006

Nick came to my office to have dental work done. My boss did a root canal on one of his upper molars and two fillings on his top front teeth. All of these were damaged in the accident. He also used a laser to trim irritated, overgrown tissue.

Nick was short fused with my boss, and I was very embarrassed. My boss was so patient with Nick. Working on him is not easy since he can't open his mouth very wide now. My boss has been very supportive. I know Nick was frustrated and sensitive, but sometimes he can be an ass.

My mom saw a surgeon to evaluate her breast on Monday, then had an ultrasound today. The ultrasound was questionable, so they want to do more testing.

Kenzie has been doing great with potty training, so Nick and I decided to set up my old twin canopy bed for her in her room. We bought her a new mattress and box spring, as well as the Dora the Explorer sheets and comforter that she wanted.

Tonight, is her first night in her "big girl bed". We pushed one side of the bed against the wall and put her toybox bench on the other side of the bed in the hope she doesn't fall out. She is so excited!

Monday, April 3, 2006

    Joe Vance started digging the hole for our garage footing today. We had started getting prices in 2004, before the accident, and now it's finally getting started. We are both so excited.

    Kenzie has been doing great in her big girl bed and with no "accidents" for quite a while now, I think we can officially say that we're done with potty training.

    I have been feeling lousy all week. I have chest pain and back pain on my left side and a cough that just won't quit. I went to the Walk-In Clinic today and they diagnosed me with bronchitis. I went to the pharmacy on my way home to fill my prescriptions for an antibiotic and a cough medication. Hopefully they work quickly!

Saturday, April 8, 2006

    Kyle, Krista, John, Gwen, Nick, Kenzie, and I went to the Relay for Life Breakfast with the Easter Bunny this morning. They served pancakes, bacon, sausage, and juice.
    Kenzie and I had our picture taken with the Easter Bunny, then decorated a foam frame with stickers and letters bright spring colors. It was a fun morning.
    This afternoon though, Kenzie caught me off guard and made me cry. She came over to me and said, "I'm sorry to tell you mommy, but my Daddy died." I told her to never say that again. I know she's just a little peanut, but that statement hit way too close to home. It wasn't until two hours later that I realized that Simba says that to his mother in *The Lion King*, and Kenzie was watching it earlier.
    My parents came over tonight to decorate Easter eggs with Nick, Kenzie, and me. My Dad never fails to make his multicolored eggs by dipping each end of the egg in a different color. This year, Nick joined in and made his eggs look like some of his correctional officer friends, complete with uniforms and badges. They are hilarious!
    Kenzie was amazed by the plastic sleeves that I bought to wrap some of the eggs. She had fun watching them shrink up in the hot water. She enjoyed dipping the wrapped eggs in her favorite colors too.
    All in all, it was a good day. Now if I could just get rid of this bronchitis!

Sunday, April 9, 2006

Kenzie yelled to us from her bedroom at 4:30 am wanting one of us to go get her and bring her in our bed. We told her "No" and to go back to sleep. She yelled, "But I can't get back in my bed!"

I got up to check on her and found her stuck on the floor between her bed and her toy box. I teased her that they wanted a Kenzie sandwich, hoisted her out of there, and tucked her back in to bed. She was totally fine with being in her own bed, just not squished on the floor!

Kenzie and I planted pansies and played Bocce ball with Nick. Later, the three of us went to my parents' house for Sunday dinner with Krista, John, and Gwen. We all colored Mom and Dad's Easter eggs together and had a very nice visit.

Tonight, Nick and I installed a bed rail on Kenzie's bed. No more 4:30am wake up calls for us... I hope!

Monday, April 10, 2006

The right side of Nick's mouth is swollen, red, and hurting. His teeth appear to be leaning backward toward his tongue like his mouth is caving in.

I called Dr. Bennett and he asked if Nick had his dental work completed. I told him what had been done and that the dentist had lasered swollen tissue. Dr. Bennett started to yell at me saying "There are to be no more lasers used in his mouth!" and "Why didn't you call me about this sooner?!"

It's a good thing that that man is good at what he does because he has NO chairside manner. He is such a jackass sometimes!

IF there had been a concern sooner, we WOULD have called! My crystal ball apparently wasn't working well enough for him! Why would he even begin to think that I wouldn't call right away?!? We call that man on any day of the week if we are worried about something. And, who died and left me Nick's boss? Nick is more than capable of calling at this point, and he HAS. So why yell at his wife?!?

Tuesday, April 11, 2006

Nick and I went to Dr. Bennett's office. He told us exactly what we were expecting. Nick's jaw is broken on the left side near his first premolar.

What we weren't expecting to hear was that Dr. Bennett is going on vacation so Nick will need to wait to have surgery until April 24th or so. The thought of him having to go a couple of weeks with a broken jaw is heartbreaking.

Nick went to work, and I went to get his prescription for Vicodin filled and brought it to him. I called his physician to schedule a pre-op physical for him too.

When he got home, Nick was totally disgusted. Who can blame him? He is in pain with a broken jaw and can't get it fixed for two weeks.

Wednesday, April 12, 2006

    Kenzie wiggled past her bedrail and fell out of bed last night. She woke up and yelled for me, so I got up and got her back in bed, tucked her in, and kissed her good night once again. So much for no more early morning wake up calls. Thankfully she didn't get hurt though.

    I called Dr. Bennett this morning to let him know that the left side of Nick's face is very swollen. He said he'll get Nick in for surgery sooner if he needs to, but he prefers to wait until he has enough time to do everything that he wants to. He set a surgery date for April 27th at 10:15am.

    It's so hard to be patient when I know how much Nick is hurting. Does it make sense to do everything that Dr. Bennett needs to do all at once to prevent Nick having to go under general anesthesia an extra time? Yes, it does. Does it stink that the poor man needs to wait and be in pain? Absolutely. I give Nick so much credit. He is going to work every day, in pain, with a broken jaw.

Sunday, April 16, 2006, ~ Easter

    Kenzie woke us up this morning saying, "Mommy! I wonder if the Easter bunny came?!?! The three of us went downstairs to see what the bunny brought. Kenzie was so excited with her Dora the Explorer Gardening Set! She was adorable hunting for the Easter Eggs hidden around the house too.

    We went to Krista's for breakfast with the family. Krista and John made French toast, eggs, bacon, sausage, and a fruit salad. I love our Easter breakfasts together! The kids had fun searching for eggs too. Poor Nick only ate the scrambled eggs, but at least he didn't need to puree those.

    Mom made a fantastic ham dinner this afternoon too. Nick pureed everything but didn't feel like eating. He was in so much pain, you could just see it in his eyes. I'm sure it is very hard to sit and smell all the wonderful food and wonder if you'll ever eat regularly again, not to mention be in terrible pain while you're doing that.

    My chest feels so heavy tonight. Though today was very nice, yesterday was even better because Nick and I had a chance to have some time to relax and fish from our jon boat. We both really needed that.

Tuesday April 18, 2006

My mom had five biopsies of her breast today. She won't get result for five days. She is scared to death and honestly, it's nerve wracking for all of us. I just pray that it's nothing.

Cary called to check on us today. She told me that Brandon told her that Nick broke a small piece of bone in his jaw.

Really? A SMALL piece? Talk about minimizing things! I can't help but think he is just trying to make himself feel better by lying to himself about what is really going on.

Then, I question my irritation. How did Brandon find that out? He doesn't call Nick at all. Did whoever told him minimize it to protect his feelings? Then again, if you're protecting his feelings, why the heck would you tell him in the first place.

My mind thinks way too much. Sometimes, when Nick is really hurting, I want to be angry with Brandon so it's just easier to assume the worse. His avoidance of us doesn't help that at all.

Thursday, April 20, 2006

  We have four walls of the new garage up! It looks awesome! I am so excited to be able to put our camper under cover at our own home sometime this year!
  When Nick got out of work tonight, he, Kenzie and I took our camper to Sunshine Campground and set it up. My parents and Krista's family are also camping here for this long weekend. Mom and Dad were already set up when we got here and were at her follow up appointment with the surgeon.
  Mom and Dad got back to the campground around 6:20pm. Dad knocked on our camper door and came in crying. Mom has breast cancer. They aren't sure how she got it; it might be the hormone replacement therapy but they're not sure. I am scared to death for her. I pray that they can get rid of it, and she'll be fine. I am also petrified that I will end up with breast cancer from all the hormones that I took to get pregnant if they think her cancer could be hormone induced.
  Krista, John, Gwen, Mom, Dad, Nick, Kenzie, and I had dinner together then went to the playground. We had a campfire and tried our best to relax and have fun. Our goal was to get Mom and Dad's minds on something else. I hurt for them.
  After I put Kenzie to bed, I felt horrible and threw up. I am a mess. My nerves have gotten the best of me. I cried myself to sleep in Nick's arms. As if the poor guy doesn't have enough to worry about, now his wife is even more of a hot mess and his mother-in-law is ill.

Friday, April 21, 2006

    Nick went to work from the campground today. He's down to 125lbs, cranky, and just miserable. Dr. Bennett called in a new prescription for pain medications to hold him over until surgery.

    Krista, Gwen, Kenzie, and I went to the playground where the girls met a new friend and played well together. That gave Krista and I time to talk about Mom and her diagnosis. Thank God she and I are always here for each other. We have had our "moments" over the years, but I never question whether she has my back or vice versa. For the most part, we think alike on how to handle things and both of us are always ready to help when it comes to our parents. I consider myself very lucky to have her.

    After dinner tonight, we sat by the campfire and made s'mores. For some crazy reason, I tried to clean off the s'more fork, still hot, with the tin foil from the chocolate bar. I burned my hand badly. I ran it under cold water then spent the night with ice on it. I've got a lot of blisters on my palm and fingers. Lesson learned, don't deal with fire when your mind is preoccupied.

Tuesday, April 25, 2006

    Nick and I went to his pre-op appointment with Dr. Bennett today. After that, we went to his work with paperwork for Human Resources. Each step we take always has paperwork attached to it.

    I was still having a very heavy feeling in my chest, so Nick stayed home with Kenzie while I went to the Walk-in Clinic to be checked over. The doctor there ran an EKG on me then came into the room to tell me that I may be having a heart attack. He gave me an aspirin and called an ambulance to bring me to the hospital. I called Nick to let him know what was happening. He told me that he would meet me at the hospital.

    I had my very first ambulance ride to the hospital. The EMTs were very nice, but I was a nervous wreck. My parents and Nick were waiting for me there. The doctors ran a bunch of tests and concluded that it was my gastroesophageal reflux and anxiety. They said that the doctor at the Walk-In read the EKG incorrectly.

    They gave me a prescription for a short-term anxiety medication and a new reflux medication too. I am so thankful that I hadn't had a heart attack. I have to say, if I didn't have a heart attack being loaded into an ambulance and rushed to the hospital, I probably never will.

    While I was waiting to be released, my mother called my office to let them know what happened and that I won't be in to work tomorrow. A half hour later, I was shocked when suddenly, Kyle was standing near my bed. His sister-in-law works with me, and she told him that they thought I had had a heart attack. He tracked me down at the hospital to see if I was okay. This man is an unbelievable friend to all of us!

Thursday, April 27, 2006

    Nick and I picked up Dad and went to Harris Hospital for 8am. When we got there, we were told that the Operating Room was running one and one-half hours late. They finally took Nick down for surgery at 11:40am. My Dad and I did our normal trip to Friendly's for lunch then went back to the Family Waiting Room to wait for news about Nick.
    Dr. Bennett called up to the Waiting Room to let me know that he was unable to place bone. There was a pus pocket on Nick's left side and the anterior bone had resorbed. Dr. Bennett removed the bone and placed two titanium plates. He finished the surgery at 4:45pm.
    Dad and I wanted to wait to see Nick, but Dr. Bennett told me that he wouldn't let us see him until 8:45pm. I felt guilty as heck, but we decided to come home so I could spend a little time with Kenzie. If we had stayed, we would not have been home until at least 11pm. Knowing that we will be heading back to the hospital in the morning, staying didn't make sense, yet feel horrible about it.

Friday, April 28, 2006

    Krista brought me to John's work today so he could drive me to the hospital to see Nick. Nick was really hurting. Dr. Bennett came in to check on Nick and said that he can't let him go home until his pain is under control.
    The "Cookie Doctor" gave us a prescription for a liquid antibiotic and pain medication. John and I went to the hospital pharmacy and other pharmacies in that area, but no one carried those medications as liquids. We had to drive an hour and a half away to get both prescriptions filled. I felt bad having John drive around, but the journey left me with a snafu that I will probably remember for years to come.
    We were driving on the highway and out of the blue, John started talking but what he was saying made no sense to me. I started to answer his questions the best way I could, only to find that he was on one of those new blue tooth phone devices with a client. I felt like a complete idiot when I realized he wasn't talking to me at all. I looked over and saw a big smirk on his face and wanted to just shrink in my car seat from embarrassment.
    My mother went to her surgeon today. Her cancer is very small, but very aggressive. They told her she has a ninety five percent chance of recovery. They will remove it and do radiation and possibly chemotherapy. She now needs to wait for her next appointment.

Saturday, April 29, 2006

Nick was discharged at 11am. Of course, they gave him an additional prescription that needed to be filled.

I got Nick home and settled in, then my parents brought take-out over for supper. I felt so nauseous, my stomach actually hurt. I had no interest in eating.

After I put Kenzie to bed, Nick and I had a chance to be alone and talk. He cried because he's so disgusted. He is in a lot of pain, and he's scared that he'll feel this pain forever. He misses holding me and Kenzie.

I reassured him that things will get better, all the while praying that I wasn't lying to him and they actually will.

Monday, May 1, 2006

  I spent the day prepping for Kenzie's birthday party. I can't believe she's going to be three! I baked her a Dora the Explorer birthday cake this morning. This afternoon, while she napped, Mom came over to help me while I decorated it. It was nice to spend the time with mom and she was a big help by washing decorating bags and tips as I finished with them. When Kenzie woke up and saw her cake, she was super excited too!
  Mom took Kenzie home with her for dinner so Nick and I could go to his evening appointment with Dr. Bennett. I realized after; I was holding my breath when Dr. Bennett looked inside Nick's mouth. Waiting to hear what the doctors have to say at this point can be excruciating. The look on Dr. Bennett's face told the story. Nick's new reconstruction plate is already poking through the tissue inside his mouth. Dr. Bennett gave me care instructions as I am once again brushing Nick's teeth for him and continuing to do the rest of his wound care.
  We are both so disgusted. We know that there are more surgeries to come, but it would be nice to have ONE surgery where it was completely successful and a step forward.
  We picked up Kenzie from my parents and came home to snuggle with her and watch TV in our bed. Our family is the one constant we have, and I thank God for that.

Tuesday, May 2, 2006

    Kenzie had a very busy day today and she loved every minute of it. Gwen and my mom came over this morning and the girls played in the Ball Pit that my neighbor gave to Kenzie. They threw balls at each other, buried each other, and giggled up a storm.

    I made grilled cheese sandwiches for everyone for lunch, then mom and I put the girls down for their nap. While they slept, we transformed the house into a Dora the Explorer party zone. We hung streamers and banners and blew up Dora balloons. The dinner table had a Dora tablecloth, plates, cups, and napkins too.

    Krista, John, and my dad came after work and brought pizza with them to celebrate Kenzie's birthday. We had cake and party ice cream then watched her open her gifts. She is one very lucky kid with all the love and gifts she received today!

    After everyone left and we cleaned up, I did Nick's care and found that his plate is more exposed on his right posterior area today than yesterday.

    To escape our frustration, he and I ventured out to the new garage to check out the second floor. My fear of heights and the open backs to the two sets of stairs are not a great mix, but it's coming along very nicely!

Friday, May 5, 2006

    Today the three of us went flower shopping. This is my absolute favorite springtime activity and I needed to have something to keep my mind off Mom's breast cancer surgery today. I am not overly artistic, but I love creating pots of gorgeous mixes of flowers, so it was the perfect distraction.

    When we got home, Nick and I put out our wrought iron furniture in the yard, then I started planting my flowers. Nick helped by planting my new hydrangea bush for me too. I love adding annuals to my perennial beds, so I get many months of color. I can't wait for the morning glory seeds that I planted to sprout and curl up my arbor.

    My hummingbird feeders were busy all day and I was able to get some videos of them flitting around near Kenzie. At one point, there were six of them by her head and I started to wonder if this was a form of child abuse. But she was so excited with a big grin on her face, I knew she was enjoying it as much as I was.

    Mom's lumpectomy surgery went well. Dad asked me to pick up her pain medication at the pharmacy and drop it off at the house for them so she would have them when they got home. She's very nauseous and uncomfortable, but she's ok. She needs to wait to get the results from the lab then she will see an oncologist.

Monday, May 8, 2006

Kenzie, Nick, and I went to see Dr. Bennett. He said that things are looking good, even with the reconstruction plate showing through. He removed sixty percent of the sutures and told me to keep doing Nick's care the way that I have been.

Nick told him that he has been dealing with a lot of frequent bathroom visits. Dr. Bennett feels that Nick may have C. Difficile from the antibiotics. He called him in a prescription for flagyl and we picked it up on the way home.

We also went to Dr. Jacobs, an endocrinologist, for Nick's diabetes. He was a wealth of knowledge and directed Nick to inject Humalog prior to each meal to help with his blood sugar spikes.

When we left Dr. Jacobs' office, we stopped at the rest rooms in the medical building before our hour-long drive home. Wouldn't you know that Dr. Case walked into the men's room while Nick was in there. He asked Nick how he was doing as a pleasantry. When we got in the car, Nick told me that he wanted to tell Dr. Case, "It's a good thing my wife isn't here right now, she'd have something to say to you." My husband knows me well. I hate what Dr. Case did to him. I wouldn't say anything to him, but I sure would be thinking it.

I don't know what's going on with Kenzie, but I think the "terrible twos" are hitting at three. She was so whiny, cranky, and fresh today, it was ridiculous. When we would discipline her, she would blow raspberries at us.

The three of us were supposed to go fishing tonight, but Nick and I decided to cancel because she was being so naughty.

Thursday, May 11, 2006

Nick went fishing with Kyle while I spent the day with Gwen and Kenzie. We played games then Gwen and I pretended to be zoo animals while Kenzie was our keeper. Kenzie loves playing "animal" and Gwen is a good sport. She was a lion, and I was an elephant today.

Mom and Dad came over after Mom's post-op appointment with her surgeon. The tests showed that there were no cancer cells in her lymph nodes, however it was a Class III cancer which was fast growing. The lab report questions whether the surgeon removed enough healthy tissue around it.

Mom will have an appointment with an oncologist next. She is scared to death. I don't blame her. I am scared for her. But just like they have been here for us, we will be there to help her get through this too.

Monday, May 15, 2006

Kenzie and I rolled more of her coins this morning and took them to the bank for her college fund. She had her annual physical with her fantastic pediatrician today. She is now thirty-eight and a half inches tall!

After her appointment, I surprised her with lunch at McDonalds and some time on the playscape there. She was super excited!

We spent the afternoon coloring and reading books together. Some of my happiest times are spent snuggling and reading to her.

Nick has been back to work for a little over a week. I think it's good for him to get out and see other people.

After work, Nick went to Dr. Bennett's. He came home very upset because Dr. Bennett told him that he wouldn't be surprised if the plate ends up showing through his tissue from one end to the other. Unless Nick has a problem, he won't see him again until May 31st.

He also saw Dr. Jacob. He is having Nick try a new diabetes pill instead of the injection. I hope it works so he won't have to inject himself so much.

The oncologist that Mom is supposed to be seeing keeps rescheduling her appointment. It's very upsetting for her to have to just wait. I totally understand that.

Since Mom's diagnosis, she has been searching for the reason. She eats right and exercises. They have now ruled out hormones as the culprit, so what caused the cancer? She has been reading that radon gas has been found to be prevalent in our town, so she decided to have her home, ours, and Krista's tested. The gentleman who tests for radon came today. We'll see.

Wednesday, May 31, 2006

After a fantastic, relaxing Memorial Day camping weekend by the ocean with my parents, Krista and her family, and Dean and his family, it's back to reality for us.

Mom finally had her appointment with the oncologist, only to be told that she should be seeing a medical oncologist not a radiation oncologist. Don't these doctors review charts before they see patients? This is getting ridiculous.

Nick had his appointment with Dr. Bennett. Dr. Bennett told him that he will see him in August. After that appointment, he may cut out the upper reconstruction plate and leave the lower plate in. He would then place bone in the late fall.

Nick told him that I am wondering if he might have sleep apnea now because I hear him gurgling and stop breathing at night. Dr. Bennett told him that there is no way that his tongue will block his airway. I find that hard to believe considering he can't control his tongue.

Dr. Bennett is also blaming the laser surgery that my boss did because Nick's tissues are so tight. I say "Bull!" My boss barely used the laser on Nick. There is no way that the failure of this surgery is his fault. Dr. Bennett is looking for a scapegoat.

Tuesday, June 6, 2006

It's been a very busy few weeks for all of us. The garage is nearly completed except for the finish work. Nick and I decided to finish the second-floor room, which will be "Man Town", ourselves. We're using tongue and groove pine boards for the ceiling and walls and I'm finishing the boards with linseed oil before Nick hangs them.

We've been buying fifty boards at a time and hanging them when they are finished drying. I love how it looks up there. The only thing I don't like is looking out the second-floor window at how high up I am. Mom and Dad have been helping us when they can too.

Mom went to the medical oncologist today. She recommended both radiation and chemotherapy. She also recommended genetic testing.

Neither Krista nor I really want Mom to have the testing as neither of us will do anything different with our healthcare. Both of us plan on having mammograms yearly now even though they are not yet recommended due to our ages. Neither of us would have a preventative mastectomy either. We also both feel that Mom would have a hard time dealing with a positive result as she would feel guilty and worry more than necessary. Mom said she needs to think about it more, and we respect that it is her decision.

Kenzie has been enjoying the warmer weather and playing outside. She has been spending a lot of time with Gwen on her new mini moon bounce too. The two of them are like little hopping bunnies in that thing!

Thursday, June 8, 2006

    Yesterday, mom got a call from the medical radiologist. She said that Mom's mammogram showed something new and questionable. Today Mom found out that there is, in fact, a new barbell shaped area. She is petrified. The next step is a computer guided needle biopsy of the new area.

    Nick's friend, Jarrod, and his wife, Jessica, flew here last night to visit for the weekend. They are great people and Kenzie loves them both.

    Today, Nick and I took them into Boston to show them around. We took them to the bar, Cheers, and Fenway Park. Kenzie stayed with my parents until we got home then she, Jessica, and I played games.

    Tomorrow, Kyle is taking the five of us deep sea fishing on his boat, so I made grinders and got together items for a picnic while we're out on the water. We're all looking forward to it and it gives me something good to think about instead of worrying about my mom and the fact that our radon test came back, and we need a water purification system installed in the house. At least the air isn't saturated with radon, that's a positive.

Tuesday, June 20, 2006

    Mom had an appointment with her oncologist last week. She agreed with mom that she should have a mastectomy. She got her in with the surgeon the next day for a pre-op visit. Things were finally moving. My poor mom has been in limbo for months waiting for appointments and results.
    Today she had her surgery. It went well and she should be able to go home tomorrow. She told me that she has very little pain. Now she just needs to get through her treatments and get well. This has taken a toll on her emotionally. Who can blame her?
    The last year and a half, there has been a somewhat constant list of crazy things happening to all of us, mostly health related. The fact that we support each other is a God send. I can't imagine getting through all of this without that support.

Wednesday, June 28, 2006

    Kenzie and Gwen were both very headstrong today and couldn't seem to get along. The only time they did was when we went out to play in the kiddie pool. Of course, there they were shooting each other, and me, with water guns so they were working out their "issues."

    Dad and Mom came over at 2:30 so that Dad could stay with the girls while Mom and I went to the hairdresser for a wig consultation. Carissa was wonderful with Mom and gave her very honest opinions and recommendations. We have seen Carissa for years and I can't imagine how hard this would have been without her kindness and keen sense of humor. She has teased me about my graying hair, my need to hide behind bangs, and numerous other things over the years. The thing that makes Carissa special, is the fact that she never hurts your feelings with her teasing because she does it to gently make you aware of what you need without telling you that you do. I absolutely love that woman, and so does Mom.

    Mom also received her results from the tissue testing from the mastectomy. She had three new spots of cancer and fortunately, still nothing in her lymph nodes. Thank God they removed the whole breast and gave her the best chance at being with us for a very long time.

Tuesday, July 4, 2006

It's been a good five days of camping at Bonfire Lake Resort with my parents and Krista and her family. The kids played well for the most part and both are like little fish in the lake.

Kenzie spent most of the weekend with her left eye swollen shut from a bug bite, but that didn't slow her down at all. I couldn't even get her to keep ice on it when it first happened because she wanted to play.

We all spent a lot of time playing games, doing crafts, swimming, and fishing. The adults enjoyed some quiet time by the campfire after the littles had their s'mores, brushed their teeth, and went to bed. One night, Krista and I had some quality sister time chatting too. I loved it!

Mom had her drain removed yesterday and was told she will have chemotherapy every two weeks for two months then every three weeks for three months. The concept is very daunting, but she needs to beat this so we will support her and help her in any way we can.

On the way home from the campground this afternoon, we had a tire blow out. Nick called our roadside assistance company and two and a half hours later, they told us they weren't coming. We were on the shoulder of the very busy state highway and every tractor trailer truck that sped by us shook the camper. It was nerve wracking BEFORE we knew that no one was coming!

Once again, Dean to the rescue! He brought his heavy-duty truck jack and helped Nick change the tire. We got home safely. Tomorrow Nick will get all new tires put on the motorhome.

Sunday, July 9, 2006

    Two camping weekends in a row! That's a new record for us! We started with setting up our camper and my parents' camper on Friday then Kenzie and I took Mom for her P.E.T. scan. After that, the rest of the weekend was spent reading, playing in the pond, and sitting by the campfire.

    I am still struggling with nausea, stomach pain, and anxiety but getting away definitely helps. My doctor has changed medications for me multiple times, I hope we get it right eventually.

    Kenzie is truly showing her love for nature as she grows. She is mystified by the tiniest bugs and worms. She loves to put her little goggles on in the pond and watch the minnows. We brought a pail down to the pond and she caught a water bug with her net. I would have never imagined how happy this "new pet" could make her.

    She and Nick tried capturing tadpoles but since Kenzie wanted to catch them herself, and she was a bit too excited, she just came home with her water bug pet. When I see her and how gentle she is with little creatures, I wonder what her future will hold.

Sunday, July 16, 2006

Another unplanned camping trip with my favorite people! This weekend we went to the ocean. The campground is nothing but a parking lot, with no camper hook ups and only bathrooms, but the proximity to the water is great.

I swear that Kenzie's favorite past time is getting lubed up with sunscreen and then doing summersaults in the sand! She was a hot mess every day and in desperate need of a shower before bed every night but oh my goodness, did she have fun!

Some of our friends camped this weekend too and they have daughters who are about 6 years older than Kenzie. The girls were terrific with Kenzie and Gwen, and they taught them how to search for tiny crabs. Kenzie collected them in a bucket to watch them move around before setting them free again. She was so animated and excited when she was lifting rocks to look for them. She talked to each one as she put it in the bucket and told them that she loved them. It was so sweet.

Thursday, July 20, 2006

I had a great start to my day when Kenzie asked to come in my bed so we could snuggle and sing and play. She is so animated when she sings, she just cracks me up!

Krista dropped Gwen off to me and both girls couldn't wait to get dressed because Cary and Elizabeth were coming over to play. We never see Brandon anymore, but Cary and I talk frequently.

The three girls played dress up and pretended to go grocery shopping with Kenzie's little shopping cart. Seeing them walk around in kiddie high heels with boas around their necks and purses on their arms was a hilarious sight to see.

Cary and I got a chance to talk while they played. Brandon is drinking a lot and gets angry with her if she tries to update him on Nick's condition. She tries to talk to him, but he just does his own thing and leaves her and Elizabeth to do theirs.

I made turkey club sandwiches for all of us then Cary and Elizabeth left so everyone could have their naps.

When Nick got home from work, he stayed with Kenzie, and I took Mom to be fitted for her prosthesis. I went with her yesterday to learn about her chemotherapy too. I'm glad she's including me in on this journey as I wouldn't want her and Dad to walk it alone. Krista is a huge part as well and it's good that we can all talk.

Today was the first time that I saw her mastectomy. It wasn't as bad as I had pictured, but she is self-conscious and happy to be getting fitted for her prosthesis. Her chemo starts tomorrow, and she will have her hair to be self-conscious about soon. This is one thing we can make better for her.

On the way home, we had a good talk, which ended up in a good cry, which ended up with a bad speeding ticket. My first speeding ticket. The officer must have wondered what the heck was going on when he walked up to the car and found not one, but two, crying women. Apparently, I was going fifty-seven in a thirty-five. I would have been fined $305, but he took pity on me when I told him we were crying over her cancer therapy, and he knocked it down to an $85 ticket.

When I got home, our new radon water system was being installed. What an expensive day this turned out to be.

Friday, July 28, 2006

    Kenzie woke up very excited to bring her Auntie Krista the Happy Birthday sign that she had colored and a red balloon. We walked next door and visited with Krista and Gwen for a while this morning. It was nice to just chill with Krista and chat while the girls played. Krista made a big deal over Kenzie's gifts too. Her little eyes danced happily as Krista praised her on her coloring skills.
    The new garage is looking great! Nick painted the sheetrock on the first floor this week after work and Man Town is almost done too. The electrician finished up today and our garage door is on and working. We can't wait to move everything in!
    Mom and Dad brought me to Nick's work this afternoon so he and I could go from there to a second opinion appointment for his jaw with Dr. Caron. Dr. Caron recommended a free fibular flap surgery including bone, skin, muscle, and blood supply. He recommended that Nick seek the opinion of a specialist in Boston. We are so confused.
    It frustrates me how Nick and I can come together as a team to work on the garage or make decisions about his healthcare, but day to day life has him so negative and cranky with me, I hate to be around him. Part of me completely understands where he is coming from with his negativity. Another part of me feels that he should focus on being grateful to be alive and the otherwise great life that we have.

Monday, July 31, 2006

This morning was spent scheduling appointments for Nick with the specialist that Dr. Caron recommended as well as Dr. Bennett. The specialist, Dr. Unid, wanted a copy of Nick's records, so Kenzie and I went to my parents' house to fax all two hundred plus pages.

Mom is doing okay. She is very depressed, but that is to be expected. I think that spending time with Kenzie and Gwen helps.

Nick and I decided to let Kenzie get two goldfish. Neither of us has ever seen a child who loved animals and nature so much, so we figured that we would let her try owning fish.

The three of us went to buy the goldfish as well as a fishbowl, rainbow gravel and a rainbow monument for them to swim through. When we got home, we set everything up with her. She was so excited!

Kenzie called Mom, Dad, Krista, and Gwen, to ask them to come over to see her fish and they did. She excitedly told them all about picking up "Cinderella" and "The Prince". I love watching that little face light up.

Tonight, Kenzie and I called Gloria while sitting near the fishbowl so they could hear "Nanny's voice on the phone". I had to read Kenzie's bedtime story to the fish as well. Those little fish are now part of the family.

Wednesday, August 2, 2006

    I worked this morning, then took an extended lunch so that I could go to Dr. Bennett's with Nick. Dr. Bennett discussed removing the titanium reconstruction plate and placing Nick back into an external fixator for three to four weeks to allow the tissue to heal. After the tissue heals, he would then put in a new reconstruction plate.

    Nick told Dr. Bennett that we had gone for a second opinion and that Dr. Caron recommended a free fibular flap. Dr. Bennett was very encouraging about our having other opinions, but he did not agree with the free fibular flap idea.

    The thought of Nick having an external fixator again feels like we are starting from the beginning once again. It's so hard to know what is the best thing to do, but Nick trusts Dr. Bennett and wants to go with him. Thankfully, Nick is willing to at least hear other opinions though.

Sunday, August 13, 2006

We've had a series of rollercoaster rides this week in many shapes and forms. I started the week making numerous phone calls to various government hospitals that treat veterans. Nick is a marine veteran, so my hope was that hospitals who treat veterans, and therefore gunshot victims, would have greater expertise in treating him. I was turned down by every one of them because he is not active duty nor is he a retired veteran.

Mom is having a problem with severe depression. She is losing her hair and doesn't feel well from the chemotherapy. She has agreed to see a therapist to help her through the cancer treatment process.

Krista, John, Gwen, Nick, Kenzie, and I drove three hours north in our campers to go to Fairieland amusement park for a few days. We rode kid size rollercoasters and teacups, walked through fairytale themed playscapes, and drove mini antique cars. The campground had a pool, so we took advantage of that too.

After Fairieland, we drove north for another hour and went to St. Nick Town. I felt like a child myself when I was able to feed the reindeer that pull Santa's sleigh. Kenzie was in her glory too. The people sized candy cane and gumdrop lined walkways added to the festivity of that very magical place. At night, we also went out looking for moose, but never saw any.

On the way home, we made one last stop at McDonald's Farmland. They had tons of farm animals and a child size village with a farmer's market, church, school, and campground. Kenzie held a baby goat and that, she has informed us, was the best part of the whole trip.

Thursday, August 31, 2006

    This month, except for our camping trip, has consisted of a lot of moving and organizing the new garage and Man Town. By moving items out of the basement, I now have room for all my holiday decorations on the shelves down there. The crawl space over the kitchen, which has five-foot ceilings and used to house my decorations, is now Kenzie's playroom. A bonus to moving the playroom over the kitchen, I can hear everything that goes on up there without having to BE there. This allows me to make meals or bake while always knowing what the girls are doing up there.
    Dr. Bennett decided to cancel Nick's August appointment and reschedule for after Nick sees Dr. Unid for his consultation. Though it makes sense, it feels like we are just postponing progress. On top of that, Dr. Bennett didn't fill out Nick's return to work papers on time, so Nick missed an extra week of work.
    I have been having female issues for the last year. I have put off dealing with them because life was too busy. Unfortunately, I think my time to put it on the back burner is coming to an end, as the frequency is increasing.
    Mom is having a very hard time dealing with her fears over the cancer. She can be a bit irrational at times and I feel badly for Dad when she is. He's very afraid of losing her and though he knows she has a good prognosis, hearing her fears makes him worry more.
    Someday, when all of this is over, I hope I can look back at this diary and see that we are all supporters and survivors. Right now, I feel like we are all just floating in limbo with glances of happiness to pull us up from time to time.

Sunday, September 10, 2006

    Cold season has hit our family. Gwen started on Monday with a cough and runny nose. By Monday afternoon, my mom had called to let me know that she was afraid of catching the cold so since I babysit for Gwen, she won't be seeing either of our two families until her chemotherapy is complete.

    On Tuesday morning, Kenzie woke up with a runny nose and turned into a little snot factory as the day progressed. Both she and Gwen felt lousy, so they took a three-hour nap that day.

    By Thursday, I had swollen glands and blocked ears, but had to pack the camper for our planned weekend away at the beach. Knowing you feel lousy and are going to be leaving home is less than appetizing, but I do love our camper and feel very comfortable in it.

    We drove two hours north to Salmon Beach Campground and joined my sister's family, her husband John's aunt and uncle, and Dean's family. We watched harbor seals playing on the rocks in the river and walked the beach. Yesterday we went to a local seafood festival and craft show where I bought Kenzie an adorable handmade plaid fleece winter coat set.

    Sick or not, it was a fun weekend. Poor Kenzie has little tolerance for the runny nose, and it frustrates me that she hates to blow it. Gwen, on the other hand, gave the foghorn some serious competition. I'm very happy that we decided to go, even though we were sick.

Monday, September 18, 2006

We have an old plan that has finally become our new project. Along with our plan for the new garage, we had also planned to install on outdoor wood boiler before Nick's accident.

Nick has been busy clearing the area for the boiler that we ordered a few weeks ago. Today he transported pea-stone from Krista and John's to level out the ground inside the forms for the cement pad. He borrowed a cement mixer from his friend and is planning on pouring the concrete pad for it this coming weekend.

Kenzie and I emptied the wicker furniture off our front porch this morning, then went to Krista's so the girls could play with playdoh, and we could visit.

Mom is feeling isolated and has thrush from the chemotherapy. She called today and was crying because she doesn't feel that any of us understand how scared she is. In my opinion, unless I was in her shoes, and I pray that I never am, there is no way that I can fully understand her fear. What I can understand is Dad's fear. He and I have both been in the predicament where we could lose our spouse way too early.

The other fear I can understand is one of losing my mother who has been my best friend for years. It hurts me to have her so afraid and not to be able to do a thing about it. We try to uplift her spirits and quell her fears whenever possible. I can't wait for the chemotherapy to be done so hopefully she will feel better and more positive.

Wednesday, September 20, 2006

    Kenzie woke up this morning and found that "The Prince" had died. She and I had a fishy funeral and gave him the royal flush down the toilet. She waved good-bye to him, and we said the "Our Father" prayer. Kids are so funny. Thankfully she seemed unaffected by his passing.

    Nick decided to pour the slab for the wood boiler today. Dad came over to help Nick, then ran to the hardware store to pick up more bags of cement when they ran out. I really appreciate the relationship that Nick has with my parents. He is so good to them, and they are good to him as well. I love it when he and Dad work together on a project. Those two men mean the world to me.

    The kids and I had visited Mom yesterday but stayed outside on the grass while she was on her porch. I think it did her good because she wanted to come here today and sit outside while they played on the swing set. Watching those two girls hug each other and dance around can brighten anyone's day.

Thursday, September 28, 2006

    Our outdoor wood boiler was delivered today. The delivery driver had amazing skills to navigate his trailer around the garage, down the hill, and into place. He had a huge hoist on his truck to pick up the boiler and set it in place. It was really interesting to watch!
    Gwen and Kenzie were in rare form today. They yelled to me at least eight times when they were supposed to be going down for their nap. Several of those times were false potty alarms and twice it was Kenzie pulling her window shade down then letting it whip up again.
    They had finally both fallen asleep for about thirty minutes when the lumber company came to make a delivery and Gwen started knocking on the bedroom window to get my attention. How can two such adorable kids turn into two little devils so easily?

Friday, October 6, 2006

I decided to do a little internet search on Dr. Unid this morning and now I wish that I hadn't. Apparently, his license was suspended for two weeks in 2005 and then he had a six-month probation period. There was no information as to why. Do we really want a consultation with him?

Today was the first time we've seen Brandon in months. Cary told him that we needed to dig trenches from the house and new garage to the wood boiler for piping, so he reached out to Nick to see if he could help. He brought over his backhoe and dug one of the trenches and helped us to shovel sand to line the bottom of it. Having him here was a huge help. Cary and I picked up pizza for all of us too.

Tomorrow, we'll do the second trench, and since John is not working, he offered to come help too. Nick and Brandon will also pour the last part of the boiler slab tomorrow.

On Sunday, Dad will come join all of us in putting the insulation and protective sleeves on the pipes, lay them in the sand then cover them with more sand. Once that's done, Brandon will gently put dirt on top to finish filling it in.

We all have aching backs after day one, I can only imagine what we'll feel like on Sunday night!

Saturday, October 14, 2006

    Gloria flew in on Thursday to spend Nick's birthday with him. Kenzie was SO excited to see her "Nanny" and so were we. Gwen, Kenzie, and I went to pick her up at the airport, and Gloria had a bubblegum microphone and Cinderella coloring book for each of them. I love how sweet my mother-in-law is to include Gwen every time she comes for a visit.

    Yesterday, Gloria helped me to pack the camper and the four of us came to Lorelei Campground for their Halloween weekend. Krista and John as well as Dean's family are camping here too.

    We all went to the Rec. Hall for some Halloween craft fun last night since it was pouring out and not good weather for a campfire. On the way back to our camper in the dark, poor Gloria stepped in a three-inch-deep puddle and got her only pair of sneakers completely soaked. Thank goodness for electric at our campsite and my handy dandy blow dryer!

    Tonight, we took the kids Trick or Treating around the campground. The girls were great, though Gwen was very timid with other kids in costumes. Kenzie even went into the Haunted House with us after spending about thirty minutes trying to make up her mind if she wanted to.

    After trick or treating, we all went back to Krista's campsite for a fire. I'm so glad that Gloria wanted to camp with us!

Tuesday, October 16, 2006

    The wood boiler installation continues. Nick and I snaked electric wires through the conduit pipes that we had laid, and the electrician and plumber have been super busy getting it ready so we can light it.

    This morning, Kenzie and Gwen were so animated when they were dancing and singing. They had Gloria laughing so hard that she had tears rolling down her cheeks.

    Once we got the girls ready, the four of us headed to the local orchard to pick apples and pumpkins. I was very surprised to hear that Gloria had never been apple picking before. We all enjoyed a little taste of a red, juicy apple while we filled our bags. Gwen and Kenzie each picked out a cute little sugar pumpkin to take home too.

    My dad came over to stay with Kenzie and Gwen while they napped this afternoon so that Gloria, Nick, and I could go to Nick's consultation appointment with Dr. Unid.

    Dr. Unid was running forty minutes late, but he was very nice. He is sending Nick for a 3-D CT scan then he wants Nick to see a different doctor who is both a dentist and a physician for another consultation. So, we are on hold yet again.

Friday, October 20, 2006

The wood boiler is up and running! We had a couple of leaks where the Pex pipe attaches to the copper pipe, but the plumber got that fixed and it is working great. Hopefully it will save us a lot of money on oil in the future once it's paid off.

Gloria, Kenzie, and I spent a few hours at my parents' house today setting up for the yard sale that our whole family will have there this weekend. Krista and I have quite a bit of baby items and clothes to sell. We do these yard sales every year and I always look forward to spending the weekend with my family. We make it fun by playing with the kids, and everyone contributes food for our meals together. Dad always puts out signs on the major roads very early in the morning, then picks up donuts and bagels for us for breakfast.

Tonight, Gloria, Kenzie and I spent time up in Man Town watching Nick hang pictures. He is really enjoying getting it to look the way he wants with lots of photos of his family and friends everywhere on the walls. Most of the photos were taken during hunting or fishing adventures and have great memories attached to them.

Sunday, October 29, 2006

    What a great weekend!
    Yesterday, Gloria, Kenzie and I made candy corn sugar cookies and foam Halloween crafts together. Kenzie also insisted that I try on several of my old bridesmaid gowns to see if one fit. She wants me to be Cinderella's wicked stepmother for Halloween since Kenzie will be Cinderella.
    Last night, the four of us took turns working on our jack-o-lantern. Kenzie loved reaching in to pull out the "guts" then separate the seeds. It came out adorable and we enjoyed the yummy roasted seeds afterward too.
    This morning, Krista called to ask if we all wanted to join them for a zoo trip. Nick decided to stay home to cut wood, but Gloria, Kenzie and I went and had a great time. Kenzie always amazes me at how much she knows about animals. She is like a little sponge when we watch Animal Planet or any other animal related tv show, but it isn't until we go to a zoo, that I realize just how much she pays attention. We were standing next to the aoudads today and she started spouting off information about where they live and what they eat. When I read the sign in front of their enclosure, she was right! She can't read yet, so I know it's all information that she's storing in that little head of hers.
    When we got home this afternoon, I made a boiled ham dinner with cabbage, carrots, and potatoes. My parents and Krista's family joined us for supper. It was the perfect ending to the weekend.

Tuesday, October 31, 2006

This morning, I raked a big pile of leaves for Gwen and Kenzie to jump in. They decided that Gloria needed to jump in too. The three of them had a blast throwing leaves at each other. The girls were all giggles when they would bury Nanny in the leaves, and she would rise out of them moaning like a ghost. Gloria is such a good sport and truly loves playing with the girls. I took some great pictures too!

Nap time was less than fun today though. Gwen did NOT want to nap. She completely freaked out and ripped the gate right off Kenzie's door. I finally got her calmed down, and both girls took a two-hour nap.

While they napped, I spent a ridiculous amount of time on the phone trying to deal with Harris Hospital, Dr. Bennett, and the new doctor's office. The new doctor, Dr. Sven, wants a particular type of 3-D CT scan. Dr. Bennett agreed to order a 3-D scan, but apparently it is not the one that Dr. Sven wants. These doctors drive me absolutely insane!

Tonight, I dressed up in my maid of honor dress from Krista and John's wedding and became Cinderella's wicked stepmother for my little Cinderella.

Gloria, Nick, and I took Kenzie trick or treating at my parents', our neighbors' and my aunt and uncle's houses. After our four stops, she was tired and ready to come home. We sat with her to check out her candy and read her a Halloween tale before bed.

Gloria is flying home the day after tomorrow. I am seriously dreading her leaving. This has been such a good visit!

Friday, November 10, 2006

 Kenzie and Gwen were so naughty this morning, I can't even begin to explain it! They were fresh and they took every pot and pan from the play kitchen, threw them in the ball pit, and jumped on them. Gwen refused to pick up toys and Kenzie shut the gate to her room, couldn't get out, and proceeded to pee her pants. I got almost nothing done before I brought the two of them to Krista and went to meet Nick for his CT scan appointment.
 Harris Hospital gave us a CD with the CT scan on it so we can take it to Dr. Sven with us. Nick and I picked up groceries, then Kenzie, and came home after his appointment.
 After we read to Kenzie and put her to bed tonight, Nick and I looked at the CT scan images. They are amazing to see. A bit scary, but amazing. I printed out hard copies of them just in case Dr. Bennett wants them too.

Friday, November 17, 2006

    Krista and Gwen picked Kenzie and I up for a shopping day today at the mall. We had the girls' Christmas photos taken then got a bit of Christmas shopping done too. We ate lunch out, then came home and we all wished Gloria a happy birthday over the phone.
    Mom had her fifth chemo today. She said she feels ok so far.
    While Kenzie was napping, I went through the mail and found a bill for the consultation with Dr. Unid. He had billed our insurance $715 for a ten-minute visit where he only referred Nick to Dr. Sven. Our insurance only paid $315. That man is a pig! His fees are ridiculous!
    When Nick got home from work, we dropped Kenzie at Krista's for a sleep over and went out for dinner and Christmas shopping for her Santa gifts. She would really like a dog of her own, but since Nick has three already, we bought her a little electronic dog that obeys commands. That will have to do for now until she is old enough to be responsible for her own animal. She does well feeding her fish, Cinderella, but a dog is a whole different set of responsibilities. The electronic dog is adorable and we're both excited to give it to her.

Thursday, November 23, 2006, ~ Thanksgiving

    Thankfully, I prepared everything for our Thanksgiving dinner yesterday, so today I could truly enjoy our family. Krista had to work this morning, so John and Gwen came over by 7:30am. John and Nick worked on the roof to the wood boiler shed in the pouring rain while Gwen, Kenzie and I snuggled and watched the Macy's Thanksgiving Day Parade on television.

    My parents came over around 11am and we had hors d'oeuvres before dinner. Today is my parents' thirty-ninth wedding anniversary too!

    I love how the smell of turkey filled the air and made the house feel extra homey. Gwen and Kenzie had made Fall place mats with their picture and leaves on them when they were together this week, and they couldn't wait to add them to the table.

    Gwen and John left before dinner to meet Krista at his parents' house, and the rest of us enjoyed a very leisurely meal before they came back to join us for dessert. We all continued my tradition of writing what we're thankful for on the tablecloth. It was a very nice day.

Saturday, December 2, 2006

    Kenzie woke up extra early this morning to get us up and moving. Today is her very first hotel stay and she couldn't wait to get going! The three of us packed up the car and followed Krista, John and Gwen, John's parents, and my parents 4 hours north to a motor inn right outside of St. Nick Ville.
    I can't begin to explain how excited Kenzie was when she saw our hotel room. Everything impressed her, right down to the free soap and shampoo. We watched tv in the room until it was time to go to our evening hours at St. Nick Ville, then we headed over. We visited the reindeer at the reindeer barn and got our picture taken on Santa's monorail.
    We ended the day with dinner at the restaurant in the motor inn and a very happy child who told us, "Guys, this was a great day!"
    Lucky for her, we have another fun day at St. Nick Ville tomorrow, and we haven't even told her about the indoor pool at the hotel yet. She is going to be super excited tomorrow too!

Friday, December 8, 2006

Nick walked Kenzie to Krista's this morning while I got ready, then he and I drove two hours to Boston for his consultation with Dr. Sven.

Dr. Sven was very nice, to me. The thing I absolutely hated, was the fact that he treated Nick like a test subject and talked about him rather than to him. Dr. Sven discussed his recommendation to use a computer-generated titanium plate that would mimic Nick's original jawbone. He asked if we had any good pictures of Nick before the accident to help him design the titanium jaw.

In conjunction with that, he recommended the radial forearm flap surgery and removal of the pectoral muscle flap. He didn't feel that the pectoral flap surgery would allow the space he would need for the titanium jaw.

It feels like these doctors are just wasting Nick's body parts. To remove the pectoral muscle, when it is now somewhat stable as the floor of Nick's mouth, seems crazy to me. But then again, I am not a surgeon. It will be interesting to hear what Dr. Bennett thinks of Dr. Sven's recommendations. To be honest, I am not impressed with Dr. Sven.

Saturday, December 9, 2006

    Nick, Kenzie, and I pulled out our Christmas tree decorations then went to my cousin's tree farm to choose and cut our own tree. He has beautiful trees of all shapes and sizes. I love the smell of the fresh evergreens and enjoy a fresh tree very much. Every year, we have a very hard time picking which one we will take home.

    Kenzie picked out her favorite tree and Nick cut it down. We paid my cousin and chatted with him a bit before coming home.

    The three of us had lunch then while Kenzie was napping, I put the bright white lights on the tree as well as my wooden garland of small maroon balls. Nick and I also took advantage of her nap to stack some wood for the boiler.

    When Kenzie woke up, we picked Gwen up and went to 4pm mass. Later, my parents joined us for dinner and Christmas tree decorating. The girls were so adorable when they helped each other hang the ornaments. I made hot chocolate for us all and it was a very nice family evening.

    Tonight, Gwen is having her first overnight here. I pushed the bed against the wall in the spare room and installed a bed rail for her too. She, Kenzie, and I snuggled, I read to them before bed and tucked them in for the night.

Saturday, December 16, 2006

    My dad and John came over early this morning to help Nick install the tin roof on the wood boiler shed. A bit later, Krista and Gwen came over too, to make place markers for the Christmas dinner table. Krista and I cut out Christmas trees from construction paper, and the girls attached pom pom balls to them for ornaments. They also used glitter glue to decorate them. The place markers are quite festive and adorable!

    Mom came over during our crafting and helped too, then I made grilled cheese and tomato soup for everyone for lunch. It's so nice to have family to share the good times with. Goodness knows, they have shared plenty of the less than good times with us too.

Monday, December 25, 2006

    I barely slept last night. The anticipation of watching Kenzie open her gifts from Santa had me so excited, sleep evaded me.
    Kenzie woke up at 6:18am and the three of us went downstairs to see what Santa brought. Santa had left Kenzie a "thank you" note for the milk and cookies, and to also let her know that he was sorry that he couldn't bring her a puppy this year. Kenzie loved the electronic dog, who she named Scamp, and the accessory bowls, brush, and leash that Santa brought for him as well.
    Mom and Dad joined us to watch Kenzie open her gifts this year too. They alternate between our house and Krista's so they can get in on the excitement. We all had breakfast together then Mom and Dad left to prepare food for Krista's house this afternoon.
    Nick, Kenzie, and I spent over an hour on the phone with Gloria, Melanie, and Joe, as well as Nolan, Geena, and Eliza. I loved hearing the excitement in Eliza's little voice too. We all miss Nick's family, especially during the holidays. I always feel bad for him being so far away from them.
    Krista's ham dinner was delicious this afternoon and we enjoyed spending time with John's family there too. His grandmother, who shares my birthday, is quite a ticket. She is spunky and spry for her age, and she just loves the kids. John's aunt, Tenille, is a complete hoot who can keep us all on our toes and laughing. It was an excellent Christmas!

Wednesday, December 27, 2006

  I dropped Kenzie off at Krista's today, as I do every Wednesday, and went to work. I had a very busy schedule, seeing ten patients and working on calling patients who were overdue for appointments.

  I picked Kenzie up at 5pm and came home to an empty house. Nick is usually home before us, but I knew he was going to cut wood today so he might be a bit later. It was dark out by the time Kenzie and I got home though, so I began to worry.

  By 6pm, my nerves were weighing on me, so I asked John if he could take a ride to check on Nick. Thankfully, Nick was fine, but then I was angry. That man has no clue how much I worry about him since the accident. He just doesn't understand how effected I am by the last two years.

  Tonight, Dr. Sven called to see if Nick had had his titanium plate removed yet. He said, "Nick's case strikes a chord with me, the chord of challenge." I'm not sure how comfortable I am with his "chord of challenge".

  Either way, Dr. Sven said he was going to work with our insurance company to see if he could get coverage for the surgeries he recommended, then he will call us to schedule another consultation.

Sunday, December 31, 2006

    While Nick was off cutting wood, Mom and Dad came here. Mom read to Kenzie while Dad and I finished wiring the lights in the wood boiler shed.

    Kenzie had a fever yesterday, so she's laying low today. I called Cary to cancel New Year's Eve with them once again. This time due to a sick kid.

    I was very excited to see Nick's face when he got home, and we surprised him with the completed woodshed lights. We ate Chinese take out for dinner with my parents, then they went home, and the three of us snuggled on the couch bed in the sunroom in front of the woodstove. We watched tv as the New Year was rung in. I can't believe that Kenzie stayed awake that late!

    Happy New Year! Here's to a healthy 2007!

Wednesday, January 31, 2007

    The month of January has been a productive one. Nick finished the wood boiler shed and has been cutting wood every chance he gets. He has started teasing me by calling me "Stack" since that is my contribution to the wood boiler project, stacking wood. We now have about eight cords of wood stacked in the building and he is still going strong.

    Mom finished chemo on January 8th, and we are all very happy that things can start to get back to normal for her. She is still very nervous about the possibility of reoccurrence, but hopefully time will prove that she has kicked cancer's backside.

    Poor Gloria fell two weeks ago, and her osteoporosis got the best of her. She has been nursing a broken wrist ever since.

    Kenzie had a cold, and she was kind enough to share it with me. This, of course, happened right after I agreed to take over ordering all the dental hygiene supplies at my office.

    Both of us are feeling better now, and today she had me laughing. I told her that I was going upstairs to color my hair. She jumped up off her chair and she told me, "Wait a minute Mommy! Let me get my crayons, I want to help!"

Saturday, February 17, 2007

There have been many indecisive moments where we questioned ourselves and what we should do lately. Mom has been very stressed out and has cancelled babysitting several times because of that. Krista and I continue to watch each other's kids, but Krista is contemplating sending Gwen to childcare so I don't know what I will do with Kenzie if that happens.

Kenzie has been pushing the envelope lately with her independence. It's exciting to see her dressing herself and learning to ice skate, but she doesn't listen to direction sometimes and yesterday that meant her falling off a bar stool at the kitchen counter and cutting the frenum of her upper lip. She screamed bloody murder when it happened, until we told her she was bleeding. She immediately stopped and wanted to see herself in the mirror. That child never ceases to amaze me.

Nick and I continue to work on building our wood resources. He now has me using the log splitter too.

Today, the three of us went to Nick's appointment with Dr. Bennett. He arrogantly disregarded the 3-D CT scan photos that I printed out for him. He recommended putting Nick back into an external fixator for four to eight weeks, then placing a new titanium plate and possibly bone. He told us that he may need to do the radial forearm flap too, but he is unsure.

After Nick's appointment, the three of us went to the Harris Civic Center for the annual Hunting and Fishing show. After walking around, Kenzie felt lousy from yet another cold, so she and I stayed home tonight while Nick went to a hunting banquet with some of his friends.

Saturday, February 24, 2007

    Nick and I have spent the last week preparing for tonight. He has been wanting to share Man Town with our friends, so we have cleaned, mounted a tv on the wall, and prepared a ton of food. He has a pool table, futon, table, and chairs up there too, so it should be a comfortable place to entertain.

    Everyone started arriving around 5pm and we had a great time laughing and playing pool. Kenzie went home with Krista, John, and Gwen for a sleepover, so Nick and I had a chance to relax and leisurely clean up after the last of our guests went home.

    Brandon, Cary, and Elizabeth came tonight too. I know that Brandon was nervous about coming but, everyone included him nicely and I think he enjoyed himself. It was nice for Kenzie, Gwen, and Elizabeth to have a chance to play together too.

    Nick started a tradition of pre-drilling picture frames with hunting or fishing photos of friends in them. He then allows the friend who is in the picture to choose where they want to hang their photo on the wall or slant of the ceiling. He bows down and hands them the hammer in a hilarious ceremony. He was quite a hit!

    Cary asked me to go with her to her new house tomorrow to see the building progress. We decided to make a day of it with a visit to her house, a little shopping at our favorite country store, then lunch here. I'm so glad that we have each other!

Friday, March 16, 2007

Though the last time Nick had surgery was last April, he has had jaw pain daily. Lately, it has gotten progressively worse, so on Monday he called Dr. Bennett for a prescription for pain medication. I don't know how he lives with the pain he does but, unfortunately, he has no choice but to go on.

Nick and I went to his appointment with Dr. Bennett this morning. He couldn't see anything new that would be causing the pain. We didn't know whether to be happy or upset. We're thrilled that there is nothing new, but poor Nick is discouraged that he may just have to live in pain for the rest of his life.

My female issues continue to get worse and now I am under the care of a specialist. His opinion is that the invitro-fertilization hormones altered my system permanently. The question is, what does he do about it? He is still unsure.

I have started to help with the planning of my twentieth high school class reunion. I helped with the tenth as well. It will be nice to see my old crew.

Kenzie is spending the night at my parents' house so that Nick and I could have an Easter shopping date night. We went to the Olive Garden for dinner then to Toys R Us before enjoying a movie at the theater…alone! The only thing that could have made this night better would have been for Nick to have no pain.

Saturday, March 31, 2007

Kenzie startled us awake by running, fully dressed, into our bedroom at 6:30am. She was very excited to go to the Easter Bunny breakfast this morning.

We met my parents, Krista, John, and Gwen at the firehouse for breakfast and to have photos taken with the Easter Bunny. After we finished there, we went to the town hall for an Easter egg hunt. Kenzie was nothing but giggles when she was running through the field with us and scooping up the brightly colored plastic eggs. Once she was done, she acted like she was on a treasure hunt as she opened each egg to see her prize inside.

When we got home, I fed her lunch, and as I got her ready for her nap, it took everything in me to control my laughter. She was so impressed with herself because she could hold up her middle finger "all by itself!". I chose to ignore the meaning of that finger and said, "wow!". I figured if I made a big deal about not wanting her to do that, it would then become a game. Kids!

Tonight, we went to mass with my parents and out for dinner. They came back to the house with us and watched a movie while snuggling Kenzie. It was a good day.

Sunday, April 15, 2007

I can't believe that Easter was already a week ago! We had a great Easter from basket opening to brunch at Krista's and dinner at Mom and Dad's.

Nick had an appointment with Dr. Bennett this week and he is scheduled for his next surgery. He also has a pre-op physical scheduled with his doctor.

Friday, we came to Lakeside Campground to camp with Dean and his family. Their kids are great, and Kenzie always has a great time when we camp with them. Dean's wife, Tammy, and I both enjoy chatting and playing bingo so it's a good fit all around.

The guys went fishing a few times and Tammy and I brought the kids to the playgrounds at the campground too. Kenzie was very excited to make her first purchase ever with her own money. She bought herself a "squishy fishy" as she calls the colorful red and yellow rubber fish.

I've missed camping and getting away from everyday life. It's so easy to get into a rut when you do the same things day after day, week after week. Camping lets us all hit the reset button now and then.

Sunday, April 22, 2007

We had another great weekend of camping, but this time with my parents. Cary and Elizabeth came to visit us yesterday and stayed the entire day. The kids played in the sand and rode their tricycles while we Moms followed behind.

Nick took the girls out in our jon boat, and they both loved it. Cary and I cooked hotdogs for supper, and we all sat by the campfire and took turns reading to the kids. It was so nice to relax with Cary and simply enjoy her company.

We packed up the camper and came home today. After we were done cleaning the camper and putting everything away, Nick suggested that we take the jon boat out for an afternoon fishing session. I don't think that I have seen Nick grin so big in a very long time. Kenzie caught her very first fish! The bonus…it was Nick's favorite type of fish, a crappie!

Tuesday, April 24, 2007

    Nick and I were up by 3:15 am and picked Krista up at 4am. We drove to Harris Hospital for Nick's surgery. Krista and I waited in the Surgical Family Lounge for news for five hours.

    Dr. Bennett came out at 12:30pm and told us that it took seventy-five minutes to intubate Nick. The surgery went well. He placed three pins on each side of Nick's chin. There is one hole that extends from the outside of Nick's chin to the inside. There is also a two-inch incision.

    Dr. Bennett told us that Nick would be in a room in about one and a half hours. Four and a half hours later, he finally got to his room.

    Nick was vomiting and in a lot of pain when we saw him. We only stayed for a couple of hours so that Nick could rest.

    When I got home, Mom had already given Kenzie a bath and had her in her pajamas. After reading Kenzie a book and putting her to bed, I made my phone calls to Gloria, Nolan, and Melanie to update them on Nick's surgery.

    The fact that there is a hole from the outside of Nick's chin to the inside of his mouth scares the heck out of me. The last through and through hole didn't heal for over a year. Please God, let Nick heal.

Wednesday, April 25, 2007

When Kenzie woke up this morning, she wanted to see her Daddy. I decided to let her come with my dad and me to the hospital for the day. I packed a bag of snacks, books, coloring books and crayons, then we headed on our way.

When we got there, Nick was still vomiting since the night before. The poor guy was in an immense amount of pain. Finally, around 11am, the vomiting ceased, and he was able to keep down his pain med, chicken broth and some Jell-O.

Dad took Kenzie and I down to Friendly's for lunch to give Nick a bit of quiet time to rest. We also ran to the hospital pharmacy to fill a prescription of pain medication for Nick to take at home.

After lunch, Nick asked Kenzie to snuggle for a nap. Though that made me a nervous wreck, praying that she wouldn't accidentally hit his external fixator, it was very sweet to watch.

Dr. Bennett called me while they were napping to tell me that he was discharging Nick as of 6pm tonight. He believes that Nick is safer from infection at home than at the hospital.

So, at 7:30pm, we got home with Nick. He was absolutely miserable. He was shaking with cold, then extremely hot, in pain, and therefore also a bit obnoxious. I can't blame him. No one should have to deal with what he's dealing with.

He came upstairs, put on his pajamas, and attempted to get comfortable. I don't see a good night's sleep in either of our futures for a while.

Thursday, April 26, 2007

Dean came over this morning to stay with Nick so Kenzie and I could go to the airport to pick up Gloria. It is SO nice to have her back! The three of us grabbed lunch at McDonald's then went to the grocery store to get more clear liquids for Nick.

My dad had come to relieve Dean while we were gone, and later my mom and Gwen came over so the girls could play outside on the swing set. Gloria and I joined them for a bit too after she finished unpacking.

Nick had horrible nightmares last night and a terrible headache. Dr. Bennett decided to switch his pain medication to see if that helps. He is still in a lot of pain, but that is to be expected with such an invasive surgery. I am back to doing pin care twice a day. Knowing it hurts when I do it right now tears me apart, but not doing it would be ten times worse.

Gloria, Kenzie, and I ate supper and watched a Disney movie together. For the longest time, Kenzie was stuck on watching *The Lion King*. She is now fixated on *The Little Mermaid*. Thankfully, we are all Disney fans in this family so watching the movies or reading the books repeatedly is just fine with us.

I am praying that Nick sleeps better tonight. The surgery threw off his blood sugars, so he was up every twenty minutes last night to pee, as well as having the body shakes.

Saturday, April 28, 2007

    Nick is feeling less hot and cold sensitive today and the swelling has gone down considerably. Dr. Bennett called and I told him that I am concerned with the redness around Nick's right front pin. He told me to keep doing his care and he will check it at our next visit.

    Kyle came for a visit today. Seeing him always brightens Nick's spirits. Kyle has an awesome sense of humor and is also wonderful with Kenzie. He always gets her giggling with his repertoire of crazy accents. He is just plain great to have around.

    Later, Nick decided to try to get his blood sugars down by walking the .5-mile round trip to the mailbox with me. Battling blood sugars after surgery is always a feat for him. The pain and inflammation make his sugars go up. Elevated sugars decrease the effectiveness of the healing process. It's a vicious circle. Couple that with having a limited diet and trying to keep him from losing any more weight, it's quite a conundrum.

Sunday, April 29, 2007

Kenzie surprised us all, including herself, when she flew down the stairs from the second floor to the first floor headfirst, on her stomach! Somehow, she managed to go UNDER the gate at the bottom of the stairs and landed just shy of the couch in the living room. Thankfully she didn't get hurt. We had a bit of fun teasing her afterward because she looked like *Frosty the Snowman* doing a belly whopper.

Nick was feeling well enough to offer letting Kenzie, Gloria and I go to the zoo with Krista, John, Gwen, and my parents. It made me nervous to leave him alone, but I was also grateful for the chance to have a bit of fun.

The kids absolutely loved the zoo and Kenzie had her first pony ride. I took pictures to show Nick and called to check on him a few times while we were gone.

When we got home, Gloria and I made dinner together then the four of us watched *The Lion King*. Who wouldn't after a zoo trip?!?!

Wednesday, May 2, 2007

    Nick had a recheck with Dr. Bennett on Monday, and his endocrinologist decided to start him on new diabetes medications that day as well.
    Nick has been having sinus pain and he had a horrible headache yesterday which made him miserable. He asked me to rub his sinuses last night in the hope to decrease the pain.
    Today, Krista, Gwen, Kenzie, Gloria, and I spent the morning at the town hall for a toddler swim then we went to McDonald's to play on the playscape. It is Kenzie's fourth birthday and I wanted to spend at least part of it having fun with her.
    When we got home, Nick was feeling a bit perkier after his rough night. He and I gave Kenzie a scooter for her birthday, and she loved it. She said, "Mommy, this is my dearest wish. You made my dreams come true!" That kid is so dang cute!
    My parents joined the four of us for supper then we all went down to the local pond to fish. Gloria, Nick, Kenzie, and I took the jon boat out after Dad helped me to get it in the water. Gloria really enjoyed it too!
    I think that Kenzie's birthday was a success!

Saturday, May 5, 2007

    This is the fifth day in a row that Nick has had me up at 2:30am to rub his sinuses. Dr. Bennett didn't see anything wrong there when we saw him on Monday, or on Thursday when he took Nick's sutures out, but something is not right. His pain level is way up there. Thankfully, massaging his sinuses helps a bit.
    This morning, while Mom and Gloria helped me to decorate Kenzie's "Ariel Castle" birthday cake, Nick and Kenzie went fishing with Dean and his son, Collin. With them away, it also gave me the chance to clean the house and decorate for her Little Mermaid themed party tonight.
    We had quite a crew here tonight for pizza and cake. Krista, John, and Gwen, my parents, Gloria, Dean's family, Cary, and Elizabeth all came to celebrate. John even brought his tractor and cart over to give the kids rides around the yard. Kenzie is one lucky girl to receive all the wonderful gifts that she did. One of her favorites was a doggy alarm clock.
    After everyone left, we picked up, and tucked Kenzie into bed. Then Gloria, Nick, and I relaxed and watched tv together.

Tuesday, May 8, 2007

    I had a chance for a little quiet time this morning until Kenzie got up. At 7:30 she yelled downstairs for me, and I went to her room. She said, "This dog alarm takes forever! I've been laying here waiting for it." I guess she didn't realize that she could shut it off and therefore she scored some alone time for her momma!
    Nick went fishing this morning with Dean and Collin then came home to work in the yard. He's trying hard to keep his mind off the pain and to also lower his blood sugar levels by moving.
    My mom, Gwen, Gloria, Kenzie, and I went Mother's Day shopping this afternoon then went back to Mom's to set up a cardboard box village. The adults cut out windows and doors then the kids used magic markers to decorate them. We made a house, gas station and grocery store. The girls rode around in the Barbie jeep and made stops at each "building".
    Kenzie surprised me when we were playing. She stopped in her tracks, put her little hands on my face, and said, "Mommy, I think you're beautiful. I love you very much too." She melted my heart. I am so glad that the "terrible threes" are behind us, and we are off to a great start with this four-year-old.

Saturday, May 12, 2007

When we were at Dr. Bennett's office yesterday, he once again offered us the use of his lake property, so today we went. What a beautiful piece of property! We caught about thirty fish in one and a half hours. It was a huge lake, and we explored a lot of it from the jon boat.

This afternoon was Cancer Awareness Night at the local minor league baseball stadium, so the whole family went. It was Kenzie and Gwen's first baseball game but I'm not sure what they enjoyed more, the game or the food. Both got a Breast Cancer Awareness shaker and had fun cheering for the home team.

After the game, we all went for ice cream at our favorite ice cream parlor. The owners have been so sweet to both the girls since they were in diapers and the kids love dancing to the music of their free jukebox.

Nick is still hurting quite a bit. He amazes me how he goes on with day-to-day activities but doesn't usually complain. If anything, he gets cranky but doesn't complain.

Monday, May 14, 2007

    Nick, Gloria, Kenzie, and I went to Dr. Bennett's for a 5:30am appointment. He took impressions so he can have a nightguard made to protect Nick's upper teeth and hopefully help the sinus pain that he feels is from clenching.
    Next, it was my turn to see a doctor. I had a mole removed from my left shoulder which required many internal and external sutures for the two-inch incision. This was the second mole this year. I am seriously regretting all the baby oil and sunshine when I was a teenager!
    Tonight, I am feeling lousy. I am shaky and have an upset stomach, body aches and sore throat. I'm hoping that I feel better in the morning because I need to facilitate an office meeting. I dread facilitating meetings when I am healthy, never mind when I am coming down with something!

Thursday, May 17, 2007

Nick, Kenzie, and I brought Gloria to the airport this morning for her flight home. We sat with her for a while, then she insisted we leave because she hates long good-byes. Sadly, long, or short, we ladies get teary eyed every time.

After the airport, Nick, Kenzie, and I went to her pediatrician's office for her four-year-old examination. She is in the seventy-fifth percentile for weight and the ninetieth percentile for height.

Dr. Gorman scared the dickens out of Nick and I though. He gave Kenzie her first vaccine, and she barely winced. He gave her the second and she didn't wince at all. Suddenly, Dr. Gorman got up quickly and went to the door. He yelled to his nurse, "Doris, please come in here right away!"

All I could think of is, "What now?!?" Doris came in, and Dr. Gorman said, "Watch this." He gave Kenzie her third vaccine and she didn't wince. Doris smiled, obviously impressed, as was Dr. Gorman. He said, "This deserves M&Ms!"

When we left, Kenzie said, "How do you like that?!? I got 3 stickers, 2 Band-Aids, AND M&Ms!!" She was so proud of herself, as were we. She's one tough cookie!

Tuesday, May 22, 2007

Kenzie, Nick, and I went for his appointment with Dr. Bennett this morning. He fitted Nick's nightguard, so now we wait to see if it helps.

We then headed to my dermatologist appointment to have my sutures removed. Thankfully, my biopsy was negative.

Yesterday, we prepared for Nolan, Geena, and Eliza's visit. I put fresh sheets on their beds, purchased their favorite groceries, and cleaned the whole house.

Today, they were bumped from their flight and had to postpone their trip. We are all very disappointed. There are no available flights this week. I just hope they will reschedule the trip. It would be good for Nick to have some time with his twin, and Geena and I always have a good time together!

Tuesday, May 29, 2007

    Since Nick still isn't back to work due to his external fixator, we took an extended camping trip for the Memorial Day weekend. My parents were with us the whole time, and Krista's family was there from Friday through Monday.
    Krista's campsite was by the pond, so we enjoyed campfires there and used the campground's paddleboats. On Saturday, when we got off the paddleboat, Kenzie proceeded to vomit. The poor kid vomited three more times before she went to bed that night.
    Krista pulled a stupid campfire act, much like mine with the marshmallow cooker last year, and I ran to a local pharmacy to pick up an antibacterial cream with pain relief to help her hand. We sisters are not the brightest sometimes!
    By Sunday, Kenzie felt better, and we ventured to the waterslides. The kids loved it and Kenzie even went down once by herself without anyone catching her at the bottom! Gwen was quite the little daredevil too and we all had a great time.
    On Monday, the kids tried their hand at mini golf with the adults showing them what to do. Or so I thought, until Kenzie got a hole-in-one!
    Krista, John, and Gwen went home yesterday. I got a phone call from Krista this morning, letting me know that Gwen is now vomiting. I wasn't off the phone with her for more than an hour when I started vomiting too. You've got to love how families share EVERYTHING. Ummm....no!

Sunday, June 3, 2007

The craziness never seems to end! We were camping again this weekend. Nick and Kenzie got to the campground on Friday before me since I covered for one of my coworkers who had the flu.

Yesterday, Kenzie and I swam in the pond and did crafts together. My parents came to visit, and we all went for a walk before roasting s'mores over the campfire.

Today was when the craziness kicked in. Kenzie came into our bed at 7:30 this morning, complaining that her tummy hurt. She was holding her lower abdomen when she said it. As I was getting dressed shortly after, she started crying and yelling in pain. She wouldn't even straighten her legs enough for me to pull her pajama bottoms off, so I threw on her sneakers with her pajamas and the three of us got in the truck. As we headed to the Emergency Room, with her very distended and not bending to fit into her car seat, I was running through possibilities for her pain in my head. She had pooped last night, so that wasn't the problem. My heart was in my throat seeing how much she seemed to hurt.

About two miles away from the campground, Kenzie said she had to pee. Nick pulled the truck over to the side of the road, and I got out with her to help. That kid peed like a racehorse and as she got back in the truck, she said, "Mommy, my tummy ache is gone. Can we get doughnut holes and go back to the campground?"

We got her a dozen doughnut holes, of which she ate eleven, went back to the campground and swam before picking up and coming home. That kid may just be the death of us!

Wednesday, June 13, 2007

On Monday, Nick, Kenzie, and I went to McDonald's Farmland with Brandon, Cary, and Elizabeth. We were only there for fifteen minutes, when Brandon realized that Cary had changed bags and his medication was in the bag that they had left home. He left to get his medication and didn't return for two hours.

The kids had fun milking a goat and playing in the farm town. When Brandon got back, the two dads played on the splash pad with the kids while we moms took pictures.

Yesterday, Mom, Dad, Gwen, Kenzie, Nick, and I went strawberry picking. We picked eighteen pounds of strawberries, then I made jam. Nick was very cranky with Kenzie. Sometimes I think he forgets that she is only four because she can act mature for someone her age. His expectations can be unrealistic and when she doesn't meet them, he's pretty tough on her with his comments. I had a talk with him about it tonight.

This morning, Kenzie woke me up, sobbing, at 4:22am. She had had a nightmare that she was naughty, so we left her somewhere. I reassured her that we would never leave her because we love her.

After I got out of work, the three of us went fishing on the jon boat. We were all in a better mood, we caught a bunch of fish, and enjoyed each other's company. Relaxing together makes all of us realize how lucky we are.

Tuesday, June 19, 2007

We had a nice Father's Day weekend last weekend camping with Dean and his family. Kenzie and Nick won the Father-Daughter Fishing Derby!

Today, Nick and I went to his appointment with Dr. Bennett. Nick has a pin sticking through bone and into his mouth under the right side of his tongue. Dr. Bennett will bring Nick into his office ten days prior to his next surgery in August to remove that pin so the tissue can heal.

When we got home, we went fishing for an hour. Nick and I have been arguing a lot. Most of it is because he has been drinking beer quite a bit and hasn't been taking his diabetes seriously lately. His health is so fragile, and it irritates me to no end that he would jeopardize things just because he enjoys a few drinks. I can't imagine life without him, but I am so tired of living with a man who's so mad at the world that he drinks to avoid it.

Deer on a Tote Road

Tuesday, July 3, 2007

    I have agreed to working a second day at my office, so I now work Mondays and Wednesdays. That made me feel very rushed last night to finish packing the camper to head north for the fourth of July holiday.

    This morning, I was still stressing about getting us out of the house and on the road. Nick and I ended up having a huge argument. He told me that he's turning into what I want him to be, he's not himself anymore. He feels like he doesn't have anything since the accident because I won't let him hunt. I knew what he meant, but I couldn't help but feel hurt that he doesn't feel he has anything without hunting. He's not who I want him to be either. He is very bitter and tends to have outbursts when he's upset. The way he looks at me when he's angry makes me want to shrink and hide.

    I am petrified for him to go hunting, but I told him that I will try to work on that. After all, if he had been in a serious car accident, I wouldn't keep him from driving again, would I?

    I cried a lot, but we still left at 10am with the car in tow. I think we needed to get our feelings out in the open so that we can move on. Hopefully this camping trip brings us closer again. The three of us are camping lakeside for three nights, then joining the rest of my family at another campground for four more nights.

Friday, July 11, 2007

Kenzie gave us a run for our money during the first four days of our vacation. She was acting very spoiled and wanted us to buy all kinds of trinkets for her. When we told her "No", she had no problem telling us how disappointed she was in us. Needless to say, that child had several trips to her bunk for "time-outs".

Things got better by Sunday, and we finally got to enjoy our trip. We went to a Trading Post that had a black bear show which was absolutely amazing!

We also spent a day at Fairieland with Gwen, Krista, John, and my parents. Since the girls are getting bigger, they can ride all the rides there now. It was a lot of fun!

We all enjoyed spending time at the campground by the river, except for Gwen, who got knocked over and sat down hard in the water when an overly excited Kenzie went flying by her and knocked her over. The look on Gwen's face was one of shock, then disgust. I felt so bad for her yet wanted to laugh. All in all, it was a good vacation!

Tuesday, July 31, 2007

At the beginning of July, we helped my parents install a good-sized inflatable pool. Kenzie has been taking swim lessons and the pool has been a perfect place for her to practice. Mom and Dad love having the company and we have spent a great deal of time there.

The whole family also piled into my parents' motorhome and went to the ocean for the day last weekend. It was a perfect beach day, and the water there is shallow for quite a way out. The kids made sandcastles and waded in the water then took a nice long nap in the camper in the afternoon, allowing the adults to read and relax by the water.

Nick and I went to Dr. Bennett's office this afternoon. Dr. Bennett removed the pin that was sticking through the bone on Nick's right side and let Nick take the pin home. He only used local anesthesia to remove it. By the time we got home, Nick's entire right side of bone fragments and tissue had collapsed in toward his tongue. Once again, more setbacks.

Nick is in a lot of pain tonight. This day was so disheartening. I am glad that the next surgery isn't too far into the future.

Saturday, August 11, 2007

    The whole family went to Windy Picnic Waterslides today. It's a beautiful spot on a reservoir with lush lawns and a small snack bar. Krista, John, and I took turns going down the waterslides with the two girls while Nick and my parents watched.

    Later, while the kids napped, Krista and I went snorkeling in the reservoir. She found some beads in one spot and decided to try to collect as many as possible then use them to make a bracelet. They were pretty beads, and not too deep under the water, so I helped too. We were pretty happy with her find.

    When we finished swimming, and the girls woke up from their naps, we all went to the snack bar for ice cream. Imagine our surprise when we saw a bracelet, made from the same beads, in the gumball machine for twenty-five cents! Krista and I laughed so hard there were tears running down our faces. At least we both got a good workout diving for her beads!

    Tonight, Nick was very cranky, so I asked him what was wrong. He told me that he felt bad that he hadn't bought an anniversary card for me for our anniversary tomorrow and that he was frustrated with watching John take his daughter down the waterslide when he would have liked to do that himself. I feel bad for him. He does miss out on a lot now.

    When I have the chance to get away here and there for groceries and McDonald's or shopping with Cary, he just stays home and does stuff here. I know he's happy when I get a chance to do something, but I always feel guilty leaving him behind.

Tuesday, August 21, 2007

Kenzie had a sleep over at my parents' house last night so that Nick and I could pick Krista up at 4:30am and head to Harris Hospital.

Dr. Bennett spoke to us, and the anesthesiologist put a rubber tube up Nick's nose once again while he was awake. They brought him down to surgery at 7:45am, and Krista and I waited in the Family Lounge.

We read and chatted, then I gave my cell phone number to the volunteer in the Lounge so that Krista and I could grab some lunch at Friendly's. At 1:45pm, the nurse called from the operating room to let me know that Dr. Bennett was harvesting bone!

Dr. Bennett came out to speak with us at 4:15pm. He told us that he had harvested bone from both front hip regions. He placed a reconstruction plate, then the pulverized bone in a dissolvable mesh pouch beside it. The mouth was solid with no holes! Nick has a morphine pump attached to each hip to help with the pain.

Krista and I went to have a bite to eat for supper, and by the time we finished, we got a call that we could see Nick.

He looks good! He lost a lot of blood, so they are monitoring his hematocrit levels, but otherwise he has no nausea thanks to the patch that the anesthesiologist placed prior to surgery. If only the other anesthesiologists had done that for the other surgeries!

Krista and I came home at 7pm. I had a lot of phone calls to make to family and friends. I am so happy that I finally have good news to share after a surgery!

Thursday, August 23, 2007

Dad and I went to the hospital together both yesterday and today. Nick has done better with this surgery than any other. Though he is in a lot of pain, he was up and walking yesterday so today they released him by 11am.

When we got home, he decided that the couch bed would be the most comfortable since we can raise his head up on it. I rearranged the sunroom so that the tv would be in a good position and got Nick settled in.

I made chicken soup for supper and Nick was able to eat some. I called Cary to let her know that Nick was home, and Brandon answered the phone. At least he asked how Nick is. I couldn't help but think about the fact that he still doesn't want Cary to tell him anything about Nick.

Dr. Bennett called twice today to check on Nick. I appreciate knowing that he's just a call away if we need him.

The pulverized bone in the mesh bag that is placed against the titanium plate is supposed to harden and become Nick's new jawbone. I am just praying that it does, and that Nick doesn't develop any holes that will jeopardize the health of that bone. My husband is becoming a walking jigsaw puzzle with all the different body parts that have been moved to his mouth.

Friday, August 24, 2007

    This morning, I helped Nick get dressed, did his care, then he and I brought Kenzie to my parents' house. We then went to Dr. Bennett's office for 10am.
    Dr. Bennett took out both morphine pumps and told Nick that he had twice the amount of bone that most men his size would have. I was very glad to hear that as I have been worried about whether the surgery would have weakened Nick's hips.
    Dr. Bennett said that he had given Nick two pints of blood because his hematocrit was seventeen when it should have been thirty-five. He was pleased with what he saw today and that was reassuring.
    Nick and I picked Kenzie up and came home for lunch. Between the ride, and the pain in his mouth and hips, Nick threw up. He spent the rest of the day relaxing on the couch bed.
    I kept Kenzie busy with playing games so that Nick had some quiet. I am hoping that his blood sugars will stay at a reasonable level, so his hips and jaw heal.
    Tonight, Kenzie asked to sleep with me "because Daddy is on the couch." I agreed and I am looking forward to the snuggle time.

Monday, August 27, 2007

    Cary and Elizabeth came to visit this morning. While the girls played, Cary and I had a chance to talk. She told me that Brandon doesn't want to talk about Nick at all. How selfish! I know that he is probably still feeling guilty and wants to avoid thinking about Nick, but Nick cannot ignore what happened, he deals with it every single day. He probably will deal with it for the rest of his life.

    In my opinion, Brandon should want to support Nick in any way that he can. If that means that he gets himself some therapy so he can get past this and be a friend, he should do it. I can't imagine the demons in Brandon's head between the accident and his job as a police officer. Ignoring the pain does not make it go away.

    Dr. Bennett saw Nick today too. We are all concerned about Nick's blood sugars. His fasting morning level was 168 but his post lunch was 338. Four hours after food, he was still at 257. All of this after 15 Units of Lantus and 10 Units of Humalog. Normal fasting should be 100-130. Two hundred, at any time, is too high.

    I called Nick's endocrinologist and discussed what to do. Hopefully we can get his diabetes under control quickly. He needs it to be controlled so he can heal. We can't have this surgery fail because of the diabetes!

Friday, August 31, 2007

    Dr. Bennett took a panorex x-ray on Nick today. We could see the bone that he placed on it, and we got very excited. He made Nick a new night guard as well so that it won't hit his tissues on his left side.
    Nick felt well enough to join us at our local fair this afternoon! It was so nice to go as a family. Kenzie enjoyed riding the rides. Nick and I saw quite a few people that we know too. It was great to see familiar faces and talk to people!
    Kenzie loves the animal barns. She can't get enough of the rabbits, cows, and sheep. It's so cute to see her stop and talk to them. She's asked to go back tomorrow. Nick said, "Maybe." I couldn't believe that he would contemplate going today, never mind a second day, having just had major hip surgery only ten days ago. But Nick is the type of guy that prefers to be busy when he's in pain so that he can keep his mind off it. I admire that about him greatly.

Monday, September 3, 2007

    Today, Mom and Dad joined us for a ride to the casino to check out their kid area, then on to the Harris Mall to have lunch at Rainforest Café.
    The ambience in that restaurant is so cool. You feel like you're in the midst of the jungle, with wildlife all around you. The animals seem to come alive during a rainstorm thanks to animatronics, so you hear screeching monkeys and trumpeting elephants amongst other jungle inhabitants. Kenzie absolutely loved it there!
    After lunch, we headed to Dr. Bennett's to have some of Nick's sutures removed, then went to our favorite ice cream parlor for a rich, creamy treat on our way home.
    It was a nice day and as usual, at bedtime, I read to Kenzie and snuggled with her. When I went downstairs after tucking her in, I found Nick on the phone with Nolan. Nick was excited to tell his brother that he had gotten his hunting license for the year today. To my dismay, and elevated levels of anxiety, the two of them talked about hunting for an hour.
    When Nick hopped in the shower, I called Gloria to confide in her. What I love most about Gloria is the fact that I can vent to her about her son, and I know she will love him just as much as she always has. She also shares my fears and truly understands why I am petrified to see him hunt again. We both know how safety conscious Nick is, but not everyone is as conscientious as he is. The only good thing that I can say about him hunting right now, is that he has agreed to only hunt deer on our own property. God willing, no one trespasses on our property and gives me reason for more worry.

Tuesday, September 4, 2007

    Today was Kenzie and Gwen's first day of preschool! Kenzie was beyond excited when she was getting dressed this morning, and even more so when Nick and I dropped her off at her classroom.
    Nick had an appointment with his endocrinologist this morning, then we both stacked wood until it was time to pick up the girls with Krista.
    Both girls enjoyed their first day and had a lot of stories to tell. They like their teacher and are looking forward to tomorrow.
    Tonight, Nick and I purchased a hunting license for Nolan. He is flying here to hunt with Nick for a few days and Nick is very excited to spend that time with his twin.
    I continue to do Nick's wound care every morning and night. His hips are starting to look infected, and I am concerned. I might have to call Dr. Bennett if they get any more red.

Thursday, September 6, 2007

Nick had the remainder of his sutures removed today. Dr. Bennett recommended that Nick soak in a tub for one half hour then use half strength peroxide on his hips to help the inflammation. Best of all, Nick can return to work on Monday. He is very happy about that. When we got home from his appointment with Dr. Bennett, Nick called Human Resources right away to let them know.

Nick's endocrinologist called today too. His hemoglobin A1C is 6.0, which is fantastic! This is a good news kind of day!

Cary called today to chat. She told me that she's pregnant. She was worried that I would be upset because Brandon may have ruined our chance to be pregnant three years ago. I assured her that I am not mad. Everything happens for a reason. Honestly, my biggest concern is for her. Brandon is not an involved parent and barely talks to her. I question if it is wise to have another child with him, but that is not my call, and I wish her all the happiness in the world.

We are camping at a state park near home this weekend with my parents, Krista, John, and Gwen, so we were busy the rest of the day preparing and packing the camper. I love walking around the park while the kids ride their bikes, so I am really looking forward to that. We usually camp near the pond so the view is beautiful, especially first thing in the morning.

Monday, October 15, 2007

    The last few weeks have been busy with preschool, work, and cutting wood. We were able to get away for two camping weekends with my family too.
    One of the camping weekends was a Halloween themed weekend. Kenzie wanted to dress up as Ariel from *The Little Mermaid*. We bought a costume, but it didn't have the red hair, so I bought a blonde wig for kids and used red hairspray on it. There was a costume contest at the campground and Kenzie got very excited when she won "Best Hollywood Personality".
    Our second camping weekend included a trip to Cristov's Cider Mill where we watched as apples were pressed into sweet cider. They also sell yummy apple cider donuts and other confections. A visit to the cider mill is one of our fall favorites!
    Today, Nick found out that he has an interview at the Department of Corrections' Central Office for a position with the Intelligence Unit. He is both nervous and excited! If he gets the position, it will mean an hour ride to work, but it will also mean doing something that he will enjoy. Fingers crossed!

Saturday, October 20, 2007

     Nick's job interview went well on Thursday, now we wait and see. He is very hopeful.

     Yesterday, Nick had an appointment with Dr. Bennett before work. Dr. Bennett is very pleased with how things are healing. Thank God!

     This morning, he went goose hunting with one of his friends. It's weird how that didn't make me nervous. My mind told me that geese fly, and Nick doesn't, so they shouldn't mistake him for a goose, nor should they be shooting at anything on the ground.

     Tonight, Krista and John picked Kenzie up for a shopping spree, dinner out, and a sleepover. Nick and I went to my twentieth-class reunion. We sat with one of my best, guy friends from high school and his wife, as well as a friend of mine from grade school and her husband. There was a nice buffet, and I did a lot of dancing. It was fun to reminisce and laugh. I really enjoyed it!

Wednesday, October 31, 2007

This was a very special Halloween! Nolan, Geena, and Eliza flew here yesterday so we spent it with them!

We ladies got up early and headed to the zoo for the better part of the day. It was fun to show Eliza and Geena around our favorite zoo, and we were able to watch the zookeepers weigh and bathe the elephants too.

Nick had to work since he has missed so much in the last few years since the accident. Nolan stayed home to wait for Nick, then the two of them went deer hunting on our property. Kyle let Nolan borrow his extra tree stand, and the two of them set up close to each other. This was the first time that Nolan has hunted in our state, and it meant a lot to Nick to have him here.

Tonight, the six of us went trick-or-treating together at our neighbors, my parents', and our favorite ice cream parlor. The owners of the ice cream parlor had dressed up for Halloween too. The look on the kids' faces when they saw a full-grown man wearing a soiled diaper was priceless.

The kids got along very well and had a lot of fun together. I'm so glad they came!

Thursday, November 1, 2007

    I sat bolt upright in bed, woken up out of a deep sleep, by a gun shot. I thought I would vomit, just waiting until I saw the guys walk out of the woods and seeing that they were okay. Nolan had shot an eight-point buck. Nick was very excited for his twin, especially because he has always told him how good the hunting is here.
    The two guys decided to butcher the deer today since we are all going camping tomorrow. While they did that, I took Geena, Eliza, and Kenzie to Mariners Village. We shopped, ate at a famous pizza place, and visited Cristov's Cider Mill too.
    Kenzie is starting with another cold, so she was cranky and full of mucus for the better part of the day. Blowing her nose, as usual, was an act of Congress.
    Tonight, I made baked chicken with brown potatoes, carrots, corn, and rolls for dinner. Geena read to the girls while I cleaned up and the guys finished packaging the deer.
    I love seeing Nick and Nolan work together. They think a lot alike, and both have a lot of respect for the other. Geena and I have often laughed at just how much alike the two of them are, right down to the toothpaste splatter on the bathroom mirror.

Sunday, November 4, 2007

What a fun, yet wet, weekend of camping! The campground we went to has an indoor, heated pool and jacuzzi. It was awesome because the kids swam in the pool, while the adults took turns in the jacuzzi, or watching them. My parents, Krista's family, and some of our other friends were there too, so we had a lot of laughs with everyone.

Saturday was rainy and cool, but that didn't stop Geena and I from joining my parents and Krista at the Outlet Mall to do some Christmas shopping. The guys stayed at the campground with the kids and went to the recreation center, pool, and watched movies in our camper.

Saturday night, our group took up a whole room at the Wide Broom Saloon. It was the coolest restaurant with western saddles and horse blankets everywhere.

We finished the night with birthday cake for all the November birthdays that were in our group at the campground hall.

Today we came home, did a ton of laundry, and I helped Geena to pack their suitcases. These visits are never long enough. Though we try in entice them to move out here, Geena's parents live near her, and I understand not wanting to leave family. Tomorrow, it will be tough to say good-bye.

Saturday, November 17, 2007

The last few days have been so much fun!

On Thursday, Kenzie woke up extremely excited to be going to the airport to pick up "Nanny". That excitement lasted all day as we picked up Gloria, took her out to lunch, then had her join us at Kenzie's school for her parent-teacher conference.

Kenzie was so proud to tell her teacher about her Nanny, and to show Gloria around her classroom and the school. Later, she helped her to unpack too.

Both Friday and Saturday were spent Christmas shopping. On Friday, Gloria, Kenzie, and I shopped at the mall with Krista and Gwen after we had the kids' Christmas pictures taken. Kenzie was a bit of a stinker and didn't want to smile, but we got it done and they came out beautiful.

Our Saturday shopping spree brought us into the next state with Nick joining us too. We bought Kenzie a new bicycle and a princess recliner and still managed to get them into the back of the car without her seeing them!

Tonight, we met up with my parents and we all had a nice dinner out together to celebrate Gloria's seventy-fourth birthday today.

After we put Kenzie to bed, Gloria and I wrapped presents and chatted. Oh, how I love our chats. I can tell her anything and vice versa. She is like a second mom to me, and I love her dearly.

Thursday, November 22, 2007, ~ Thanksgiving

Nick shot a nice doe first thing this morning. Kyle came over to help him hang it so that he wouldn't miss any of the Thanksgiving festivities.

Kenzie made onion dip for chip and dip, Gloria peeled potatoes, and I made the turkey, mashed potatoes, corn, candied carrots, cranberry sauce, and rolls. I had baked an apple pie yesterday too.

Mom and Dad joined us for dinner at 12:30pm and brought the stuffing and winter squash. Krista, John, and Gwen came later for dessert too. We all signed my tablecloth and read what we are thankful for out loud.

Since we ate early this year, and it was sixty degrees today, I decided to take down the Thanksgiving decorations this afternoon and start to put up the outside Christmas lights. I couldn't help but scream when I moved my basket on the front porch and a mouse jumped out of the basket, onto my right breast then onto the ground. That was a heart-pounding moment!

Friday, November 23, 2007

    Kenzie, Gloria, and I worked on decorating the rest of the house for Christmas. In this house, that is no small feat. I take down many of the everyday items, like soap dispensers, hand towels, place mats and quilts, and replace them with Christmas ones. I also put miniature artificial Christmas trees in my bedroom, Kenzie's bedroom, the dining room, and front porch. I put six-foot artificial Christmas trees in the living room and sunroom, then closer to Christmas, we get a small live tree for the kitchen. Yes, I am a Christmas nut!

    In between all the decorating, I helped Nick to package deer meat as he butchered the doe he shot yesterday. Much to my chagrin, he is planning on gun hunting state land tomorrow for the "B" season. I am very afraid and upset with his decision.

    Tonight, the four of us, Krista's family, and my aunt and uncle, went to Paradise Restaurant to celebrate my parents' 40th wedding anniversary. We had a nice dinner together. I'm very proud to have parents who have been married so long.

Tuesday, November 27, 2007

This week, Nick started a trial period at Central Office. His first day of orientation went well yesterday and he really thinks that he's going to like it. Hopefully, they like him too, and he gets to stay up there.

While the kids were at school this afternoon, Gloria and I worked on setting up my Christmas village. She offered to stay home to watch Kenzie after school so I could meet Nick at Dr. Mallon's office near Harris Hospital. Nick had hit his shin with a log while stacking wood back in the spring, and the lump that he developed never went away. Dr. Bennett recommended that Dr. Mallon check it out.

The doctor feels that Nick should have an MRI of the right shin to decide what to do with the tumor that is there. He is ninety-five percent sure that it is benign, but he wants to be certain before deciding if it should be removed. He scheduled Nick for an MRI on Saturday.

Saturday, December 1, 2007

  Nick made me beyond happy this morning when he told me that he wasn't going hunting today. Instead, the four of us went shopping, out for lunch, and then to Nick's MRI appointment.
  This afternoon, we took Gloria to help us choose our Christmas tree. We chose a small Fraser fir that is almost as wide as it is tall. It smells wonderful!
  We came home and I put my white lights on it then made homemade cheese pizza for supper. While the pizza was baking, I pulled out all our favorite ornaments. After dinner, we played Christmas music and decorated the tree. We watched *Frosty the Snowman* and *Rudolph the Red-Nosed Reindeer*.
  I love that Gloria was here to share this day with us. She has a great sense of humor and family means the world to her. Most of all, Nick gets to enjoy a bit of the holidays with his mom.

Wednesday, December 5, 2007

When I got home from work tonight, Nick, Gloria, Kenzie, and I went to the park to see their Christmas light display before we ate dinner. Later, my parents came to visit and to say good-bye to Gloria as she is leaving tomorrow.

Cary called tonight. Her grandfather passed away and she asked if I could babysit Elizabeth for the wake and funeral. I told her "Of course" and told her to please share my condolences with her folks as well.

Dr. Mallon called Nick to say that the lump on his leg appears to be fluid filled. He scheduled Nick to go to his office next week to have it drained.

I have very mixed feelings about Gloria leaving tomorrow. It's been five weeks since we've had a week alone as a family since Nolan, Geena and Eliza left just before Gloria came. It will be nice to get back to normal, but I really enjoy having her here.

Thursday, December 13, 2007

    I am seriously enjoying this Christmas season! This is the first year that Kenzie is old enough to really help with the cookie baking. We have made brownie bites, candy cane cookies, apple oatmeal cookies, and orange cream brownies in the last few days.

    Today, we made sugar cookies. I was so proud of Kenzie! I made the dough and rolled it out, then she cut out the cookies and laid them on the greased cookie trays all by herself!

    Once the sugar cookies had cooled, I made frosting for Kenzie, and she did a great job decorating the little reindeer, trees, snowmen, and stockings.

    My mom and I have made Christmas cookies every year since I was a little girl. Since I left home, we still individually each make seven kinds of cookies and about eight dozen of each kind. We then package half of each kind and swap with each other so we can make cookie trays as gifts. It means a lot to me to carry on that tradition with my little peanut.

Thursday, December 20, 2007

Today is the third anniversary of the accident. Cary and I spent the day running errands together with the two kids. We talked about that horrible time of course and we both feel the same way, this time in December always makes us feel uptight.

After errands, we came back here, and the kids exchanged Christmas gifts. I am just happy that our friendship is still intact after all that we have been through. We understand each other and our anxieties, and that is worth its weight in gold to me.

On a good note, Nick called from Central Office today…he got the job!! I am so excited for him! This means he gets to help with investigations and more importantly, for me anyway, he gets to stay away from inmates. The thought of him working near inmates and possibly getting punched in the jaw scares the dickens out of me. At least this December 20th was a good one!

Monday, December 24, 2007, ~ Christmas Eve

  This morning I cleaned the house and made cookie trays for tonight and tomorrow. At 3:30pm, my parents picked the three of us up for 4pm mass. We went to a new church this year and the music was wonderful! I love Christmas music, but when an entire church sings along, there's something magical about it.

  After church, we came home and had Mom's meat pie and our homemade bread and butter pickles for supper. This was the first meal in a very long time that Nick didn't use his Magic Bullet blender! We ate cookies for dessert and watched Santa's progress around the world on the computer via the *Norad Santa Tracker*.

  Nick and I decided to let Kenzie open our gifts for her tonight. She loved her stuffed princess rocker and her Barbie laptop computer.

  As *Norad* showed that Santa was approaching, Kenzie excitedly put out his milk and cookies and nine carrots for his reindeer. She ran up the stairs, brushed her teeth and hopped into bed. As we tucked her in, she said, "Please don't stay up too long or Santa won't come."

  I wish we could bottle these moments and keep them for a lifetime.

Tuesday, December 25, 2007, ~ Christmas

Kenzie woke up at 3:30am, having trouble sleeping. I gave her water, and let her use the bathroom, and as she got back in bed, she said, "It's so bright out! Santa won't have any trouble finding us tonight, Mommy!" I tucked her back in bed, then climbed in next to Nick. Then I couldn't sleep either.

When Nick and I got up at 7:30, Kenzie was still out like a light. We finally woke her up at 8am because we're nothing but kids ourselves and we simply couldn't wait any longer. She peeked into the sunroom and her eyes lit up. She was so excited over her gifts from Santa!

Nick made pancakes for breakfast, and the three of us watched the Christmas Parade on TV. When it was over, we got dressed and went to Krista's for a tasty ham dinner. My parents were there as well as John's parents. Gwen and Kenzie told each other all about what Santa had brought them and had fun playing together.

When we got home tonight, I asked Kenzie if she had had a good Christmas. Her response was, "Yes! You know what my favorite part was? Being with my family, that's my favorite part!" God, I love that kid!

December 31, 2007, ~ New Year's Eve

    Kenzie and I made a cookie tray and onion dip for chip and dip tonight. We set up the food table, got the snacks ready, and got dressed for our guests. My parents, Krista, John, Gwen, Dean, Tammy, Collin, and Monica came to celebrate the New Year with us.

    We ordered pizzas and the adults sat at one table with the kids at another. The kids played great together! I had purchased tiaras for the girls and a top hat for Collin. They had fun with the noisemakers, and I had *Dick Clark's Rockin' New Year's Eve* playing on the TV.

    Kenzie kept bowing and asking Collin to dance. He wanted NOTHING to do with it and we couldn't help but laugh inside at the effort they were both putting into it.

    Everyone left by 11:30pm. The three of us quickly put on our pjs and rang in the new year watching tv in my bed. Kenzie was so cute and happy.

    2007 was a year of changes. Kenzie has grown so much and was eager to go to Preschool. She absolutely loves it.

    Nick had his external fixator put on in April and removed in August. He now has a jawbone and has eaten Chinese food and pizza without blending it in the last two days.

    I left home for a weekend in November to go to Florida with my office for a conference, and I truly enjoyed myself. I've become a tiny bit more laid back, and I really appreciate what I have in Kenzie and Nick.

    Nick is much happier at work having just received the new job within the last month doing background investigations and fingerprinting. I think he and I both finally feel that it's okay to look ahead to the future. There is a light at the end of his reconstruction tunnel. We're even debating buying him a new car.

    It's amazing how much Kenzie has changed and learned so much. She's very smart, though her mouth can be at times too. When she's in a good mood, we have such wonderful times together.

Our families are doing well. Gloria had a fractured wrist in the spring, but still visited in May and November. Nolan, Geena, and Eliza came in November and Eliza has grown so much too. Gwen has come out of her shell a bit and loves school. Dad is concerned because a house he built isn't selling. Mom is still very worried about her health; the chemo took its toll on her emotionally as well as physically.

    My wish for them in 2008 is to recognize how lucky they are and to just enjoy their lives. My goal is to remember that I have everything that is important right here beside me as I lay in this bed, welcoming in the New Year.

February 29, 2008, ~ Leap Year

    The first two months of the year have been busy but fun-filled too. Nick and I have stacked multiple cords of wood and he has now started milling some wood with his chainsaw as well.

    Kenzie is loving school, and Mom and I have started taking her and Gwen to the town hall pool twice a week. It's part of a package that the town hall runs, and it makes it very reasonable. Both girls love it!

    We've had a few rough spots with Kenzie, I think her four-week-long cold didn't help. One night in particular was heartbreaking. Nick and I have snuggled with her and read to her every night since she was born, with the exception of the nights he was in the hospital and she was read to by my parents or Gloria. We had really started reading to her when she was still in my belly. Well, this one night, Kenzie told Nick that she doesn't want him to read to her anymore because she doesn't like his voice. I felt so bad for Nick. Damn Brandon!

    Our whole family, as well as John's parents, had a weekend getaway at a hotel with a built-in water park. Kenzie amazed us by going down the big waterslides alone too! The lazy river was one of my favorite things to do as well.

    My new goal is to finish reading the "Official Guide to Walt Disney World" so that Mom, Krista, and I can start planning our trip. I am so excited to see the two girls in Disney!

March 3, 2008

After I dropped Kenzie and Gwen at school this afternoon, I drove to Dr. Bennett's office to meet Nick when he got out of work.

Dr. Bennett feels that he should extract two of the teeth that Nick still has on the lower right as the bone they are in is no longer supporting them. He will then set up a consultation appointment between Nick, him, and Dr. Carter.

Dr. Bennett wants to place three dental implants in May and let Nick heal for two months. After that, he would extract two more teeth on that lower right, place another implant in that area, and release the pectoral muscle from Nick's neck. The goal with all of this, is to eventually get Nick into a full lower denture that is supported by implants.

Right now, Nick's upper teeth are fine. His once beautifully straight teeth are very crooked from the gun blast, but they are healthy. His lower teeth, what is left of them, are barely held in place making it difficult to chew. That, coupled with the lack of tongue movement, makes eating a very laborious job.

The plan is to place implants in the new bone that was taken from Nick's hips. The future denture will snap into the implants to give Nick a stable chewing surface. Unfortunately, he would never be able to wear a denture without the implants because his new jaw line is not smooth. A denture needs that to stay in place with a sort of suction.

As a hygienist, looking into my husband's mouth is absolutely heart wrenching. It doesn't resemble the mouth that I have cared for in the past in any way, shape, or form.

Sunday, March 23, 2008, ~ Easter

    We are now on day three of Kenzie making her bed all by herself. She does a pretty good job, especially considering she was super excited to get downstairs to see what the Easter Bunny brought her this morning!

    She loved her "swim baby" and new diary. We hunted for Easter eggs then picked up my parents and followed Krista, John, and Gwen to the casino for the breakfast buffet.

    We all loved the variety of food there! They had everything from French toast and bacon to a huge fruit bar, to steak and eggs and a pastry station. It's a good thing we weren't planning to eat again until tonight because I couldn't have fit anything else in my stomach.

    After breakfast, we walked around the casino, Kenzie and Gwen skipped around, checking out the beautiful Easter decorations. They even had a four-foot-tall chocolate bunny there!

    Tonight, we had pizza for supper and eclairs for dessert at my parents' house. We hid eggs there for the kids to find too. I'm so glad those two have each other!

Friday, March 28, 2008

    When Nick went to his extraction appointment with Dr. Bennett on Tuesday, Dr. Bennett decided to extract all four teeth at once instead of staggering it. For pain, he told Nick to take four ibuprofen every three to four hours. He also told him to "scrub and beat up your gums". That last comment threw me for a loop as I have never heard of such a thing, especially after extractions.
    On Wednesday, Nick was so miserable that he got home from work at 4pm, put on his pajamas and went to bed. Kenzie and I found him still sleeping when we got home at 6:30pm.
    Today, while Nick was at work, Kenzie, Gwen, and I had a "spa day". I warmed up their little bathrobes in the dryer then they put them on. I gave them each a foot massage then soaked their feet, dried them, and painted their toenails. I put fresh cucumber slices on their eyes while they sat in their little recliners, and I painted their fingernails. Once their nails dried, they put on pretty dresses, I French braided their hair, and put a bit of blush on their cheeks for a glamourous photo shoot. There were lots of giggles and I think I can safely say, lots of memories were made.
    When Nick got home, he was still really hurting. I called Dr. Bennett. He didn't want to prescribe anything for pain and said he thinks Nick was being a "Male puss". What an idiot! I called my boss and he called in a prescription of Tylenol with codeine. I ran to pick it up, and it seems to be helping. Thank God!

Wednesday, April 16, 2008

When I went to Krista's to pick up Kenzie after work today, I walked in on Gwen pulling Kenzie off the couch by her feet. Then she hit Kenzie. I wanted to laugh at the scene but didn't for obvious reasons. It's just good to know that Kenzie is not the only one who has those kinds of days!

Nick, Kenzie, and I went to the consultation appointment with Dr. Bennett and Dr. Carter tonight. They decided that Dr. Carter will remove a lump of excess tissue under Nick's chin, as well as sever the pectoral muscle from the neck and remove the skin graft that covers it. He will close Nick's neck back up like it was before the pectoral muscle surgery, except for a scar.

Dr. Bennett will make a vestibule, or space, between Nick's gums and cheeks, place implants, and re-use the skin graft from the neck to cover the implants. The implants need to be left under the tissue for a couple of months to let things heal. Hopefully, this will all be done at the next surgery in May.

When we got home tonight, I called Gloria to update her. I am happy she will be here when that surgery happens since she comes every May and November.

Thursday, May 1, 2008

Kenzie woke up early, super excited to be picking up her Nanny at the airport today. She kept pushing me to leave so we ended up at the airport forty-five minutes early.

When Gloria got off the plane, Kenzie was wiggling up and down until she could get close enough to hug her. Once we grabbed Gloria's luggage, we surprised her with picking up McDonald's for lunch and bringing it to Nick's work so she could see him too. There, we met the Deputy Commissioner of the Department of Corrections as well as Nick's other coworkers.

After our visit, we came home and Gloria unpacked. Kenzie was all over her today, hugging and kissing her every chance she got. It was so sweet.

I ran to the school tonight for my Parent-Teacher Conference. Mrs. Connor told me that Kenzie is doing great, but that she wants to separate Kenzie and Gwen in the Fall. Apparently, the girls only want to play together and block other kids from joining them. Mrs. Connor feels that putting the girls in separate classes in the Fall would benefit them both. Though it makes me sad, it does make sense.

Cary called me to ask if I could be on standby on May 8th to watch Elizabeth in case she goes into labor. Of course, I told her yes!

Saturday, May 3, 2008

Yesterday was prep day for Kenzie's fifth birthday party. Krista and Gwen spent the day here helping us to set up and frost the Scooby Doo cake. They brought over Gwen's small Moon Bounce, and we set it up in our living room after we moved all the furniture. Gloria made the kids' day by jumping in the moon bounce with them. She is such good sport!

This morning, Kenzie made her bed and got dressed before I even realized that she was up. She was very excited for her party! She helped me to fill party bags and set up the party table.

We had twenty guests, including two of her school friends and their families. We ordered pizza and had snacks as well as the Scooby Doo cake. Everyone meshed well. The kids played in the playroom, played party games, or in the moon bounce while the adults chatted. I think everyone had a good time. Cary came with Elizabeth too. My dear friend is very ready to have her second child.

After everyone left, the four of us cleaned up, ate leftover pizza for supper, and played some of Kenzie's new games that she received today.

I think we can say that this day was a success! The only thing that drove me a bit nuts was Nick's smart remarks and Gloria egging him on by laughing at them. Those two have a very similar, warped, sense of humor.

Tuesday, May 13, 2008

Last night, we dropped Kenzie off at my parents' house for a sleepover since we had to be at the hospital early this morning. Before we left, Kenzie hugged us and told Nick, "I'm going to pray for you tonight, Daddy." God, I love that kid.

Nick, Gloria, and I were at Harris Hospital Pre-Op by 5:20 this morning. Nick went into surgery at 7:45am. Gloria and I went to the Family Lounge to wait.

Dr. Bennett came up at 10:30 to tell us that he could only place three implants due to lack of room in good bone. The partial pectoral muscle removal portion of the surgery went well. Dr. Bennett also gave me the prescriptions that we needed to fill to take Nick home.

Gloria and I went to the hospital pharmacy to fill the prescriptions, then to Friendly's for lunch. We went back to the Family Lounge to wait until we could see Nick. The volunteer then walked us down to see him and he looked great! He even joked with us.

Dr. Bennett came in to check on Nick and said we were taking him home today. I couldn't believe it! We got him home by 4:30pm and got Nick settled in.

Gloria called Melanie and Nolan to let them know, and my parents brought Kenzie home. Kyle and Cary called to check on Nick too.

I can't help but be amazed at science and technology. The surgeries that Nick has had, so far, to put him back together are beyond my imagination.

Tuesday, May 20, 2008

    Nick, Gloria, Kenzie, and I made our second trip to Dr. Bennett's office since Nick's surgery. On the first trip, he only looked to be sure that things looked okay and sent us home. Today, he took Nick's stitches out and things are looking good.

    The four of us went out for lunch, then to Kenzie's five-year-old checkup. We spent a bit of time at the park, then drove to the airport to see Gloria off.

    I hate to see her go. Though we occasionally irritate each other, we share a lot of confidences and ultimately, she is one of my best friends. I know that when she's here, or when I am at her house, we are totally comfortable in our surroundings, and if we're not, we say it. There's not a lot of people in this world who you can do that with, so when you have it, you need to appreciate it.

Tuesday, June 30, 2008

It's been a very busy month and a half. We've been camping on three occasions and on the last trip, Kenzie had her first river tubing adventure. We made a sling with a beach towel over the center of the tube to help her from falling through. She loved it!

On the second trip, Kenzie caught tadpoles and kept them in a bowl on our front porch. She checked on them every day, watching their progression as they turned into frogs. That child just loves nature and all living things big and small.

We also had a chance to meet Cary's new little girl, Marissa. She is an adorable baby and a pleasure to hold. Her chubby little cheeks just make you want to squeeze her in a big hug.

Nick went back to work two weeks after his last surgery and Kenzie finished preschool. She gave her teacher roses that we cut from our rosebush on her last day. Her teacher gave every child a sand pail filled with books. That was so very sweet of her!

Today, Nick and I went to see Dr. Bennett. After examining Nick, he gave him to okay to move ahead with the fabrication of a denture as of August 1st. I called my office as soon as we got back in the car, to schedule a consultation appointment to get things started. I am hoping that once Nick gets a denture, he will be able to eat a bit easier. Fingers crossed.

Thursday, July 9, 2008

What a week it has been! We flew out to visit Nick's family last Thursday and stayed with Gloria. We haven't had the chance to visit his childhood home since the accident, and Kenzie was beyond excited to fly.

Whenever we visit, the entire family usually gets together for at least one meal every day. There's a lot that goes in to feeding eleven people, but it's usually laid back and a lot of laughs.

On the Fourth of July, we were invited to Geena's parents' home for a picnic and swim, then to a fireworks display. The fireworks were beautiful, it was the mosquitoes that weren't. We ended up watching from inside the car with the windows up!

On Saturday, over fifty people came to Gloria's for a picnic. I will say, I have never seen people stay friends after high school like Nick's friends. It's absolutely amazing! Since none of them have seen him since the accident, it was a great reunion. Kenzie had a ball playing with the large group of kids that were there too. Best of all, she and her little cousin, Eliza, got to spend some quality time together too.

On Sunday we all went to a professional baseball game, and on Monday we went to an indoor waterpark. Tuesday was a day to relax before we hit the Marion County Zoo on Wednesday.

What do I love most about all of this? The fact that the entire family makes time to be with us every single day. It is not lost on me that they have their own busy lives and jobs. Yet, they take time off to spend with us. That's family, and I love it. Leaving today was tough, but we made some awesome memories.

Thursday, July 31, 2008

While Kenzie and I went to the beach, swam at my parents' house, and enjoyed camping for the last month, Nick has been there in body but not in spirit. I support that decision one hundred percent, because he has been hard at work studying for the lieutenant's exam at work. Today, he took the exam, and now we wait for the results.

The only break he took this month was for a very fun weekend with Dean and Tammy and the kids at their timeshares. They let us borrow one of their two timeshares and we all spent the weekend at Fairieland, eating, or tubing down the river. We laugh so hard when we're with all of them. They are some awesome people!

Nick also noticed that one of the three implants in his mouth is loose. Dr. Bennett is hoping that it will integrate over time. We will see.

I am working on a Power Point presentation for Nick. He has been asked to do a couple of inspirational talks to police departments about survival after being shot. Poor Nick is clueless when it comes to computer stuff, unless it's work related, so he asked me to do it. I have to say, going through all the surgery photos is tough. They bring back some difficult memories.

Nick sat with me for a while tonight while I worked on the presentation. He commented to me, when he was looking at the police photos, that Brandon must be color blind to not have seen his orange clothes on that white background. He certainly gave me food for thought.

Monday, August 25, 2008

My frustration level is way up today. Yesterday, the implant on Nick's bottom left came out, followed by a large amount of pus. I called Dr. Bennett, and he said to irrigate the hole with water. He was reluctant to prescribe an antibiotic.

The hole was really bothering Nick, so he came into my office so my boss could take a look. He expressed pus out of the hole, irrigated it with a medication, Periogard, and placed an antibiotic powder, Arestin, into the hole. He also called in a prescription for antibiotics for Nick.

It boggles my mind that Dr. Bennett had no interest in seeing Nick. With everything we went through, I would have thought that he would be more concerned.

Nick, Kenzie, and I went to her kindergarten orientation and bus ride. She is beyond excited to start school and ride the bus on Thursday. We are so lucky that she is!

Thursday, August 28, 2008

Kenzie woke up early, got dressed, and couldn't wait for the bus to come. It was supposed to come at 11:40am, so we got out to the end of the driveway at 11:20. We waited, and waited, but the bus never came. Kenzie was so disappointed.

I drove her to school and walked her to her classroom. She was much happier once she got there.

At least this afternoon she rode the bus home. She loved it! She couldn't wait to tell us all about her teacher, Mrs. Bunn. She has some of the kids from her preschool class in her kindergarten class. It was a great first day!

Nick had a pretty great day too. He passed his lieutenant's exam! I am so proud and happy for him!

Tuesday, September 16, 2008

Kenzie has had a head cold since the third day of school. This morning, she cried and told me that she didn't want to go to school. I know she's not feeling great, but her level of upset told me something else was going on. She finally confided in me that yesterday, she sneezed at school and boogers came out of her nose. She wanted to cry when the kids laughed at her. Poor kiddo.

When I got home from dropping Kenzie off at school, Dr. Bennett called. He was irate with me and yelling that I had no business having my boss treat Nick. He said that I was being unfair to him by going behind his back and asking for help. I told him that I feel that he isn't concerned enough to see Nick since he has gotten Nick to the finish line. I feel that he doesn't see Nick as a priority to him anymore. He told me, "How would you know, you don't come to every appointment with him anymore!" It was awful.

Dr. Bennett told me that Nick has a decision to make. Either he can see Dr. Bennett, and only Dr. Bennett, or go elsewhere. The language that that man used on me was so unprofessional and vulgar, I can't even believe he is a doctor. What an arrogant jerk! Nick CAN'T see only him! He doesn't make dentures for goodness sake! This whole thing blows my mind. And the way he says the word "Dentist" makes it sound like a swear. Does he not remember that he IS a dentist?!?

I was shaking when I got off the phone. I called Gloria in tears to tell her what happened. She's seen his arrogance, so she completely understood.

Wednesday, September 17, 2008

Nick called me at work this afternoon. He had called Dr. Bennett to ask what was going on and let him know that he can't have him fighting with his wife. Dr. Bennett returned Nick's call and apologized to HIM for the way he spoke to me yesterday. Are you kidding me? Is he that chauvinistic that he calls the husband to apologize? That apology should have been directed to me, not him. Unfortunately, after yesterday, the only positive that I see in that man is his surgical prowess. His capabilities as a person do not impress me.
    Nick, Kenzie, and I watched tv, read in her bed, and snuggled tonight. Kenzie and I are both excited for tomorrow, I am starting my new position as a volunteer in the school library. My high school friend, Erica, is the school librarian. When she saw that Kenzie was in her library period now that she is in kindergarten, she asked me to volunteer as a helper for that class every Thursday. I will be helping the littles to choose a library book. I think it's going to be fun!

Friday, October 10, 2008

  Apparently, Dr. Bennett is now going to play games. I saw his cell phone number on our caller ID, and when I answered, he hung up on me. A little while later, Nick called to say that Dr. Bennett had called him at work to change the time of his appointment today.

  Nick went to his appointment and Dr. Bennett decided to send him for a CT scan to see how things are healing. Nick also had an appointment at my office today to get his denture. I just hope he can acclimate to it without too much difficulty, but time will tell.

  My library volunteering has been fun. I have to say, it can be a little exasperating when you ask a little peanut what type of book they're looking for, and they say, "A book." I'm finding that I really need to ask questions about what they like then to go from there. I am really enjoying it though!

  Last night I went to my first P.T.O. meeting. All I can say is, I am a sucker. I got roped into being Co-Chair of Fundraising at my very first meeting. My own cousin nominated me. These people see fresh blood and go for the kill! Honestly though, I would like to help as much as I can. I truly enjoy the kids and want to be a part of Kenzie's school journey.

Sunday, October 19, 2008

On Friday, Kenzie had her first school field trip, and I was asked to be a chaperone. We rode the bus to a pumpkin patch, and Kenzie started to feel car sick on the way. The kids each got to choose a small pumpkin and they did crafts while we were there.

Kenzie's friend's dad came on the fieldtrip too, but took his own truck. He managed to lock his keys in his truck so when the bus got back to the school, he wasn't there for pick up time and his little girl was just standing there. Kenzie and I waited with her, and finally her mom came twenty minutes later.

This weekend, we went on a Halloween camping weekend with Krista, John, and Gwen. We had fun doing crafts and the trick or treating was so much fun! The seasonal campers dressed up too and had candy for the kids and shots for the adults. I had never seen anything like it before.

Their decorated sites were cool too! One street in the campground was decorated with tombstones, ghosts, spiderwebs, and "bodies" hanging from the trees. The women had dressed like witches and their costumes were very ornate. I really enjoyed it!

We came home today, cleaned the camper, and raked a big pile of leaves for the three of us to jump in. Kenzie loved having mom and dad both jump in with her.

Tonight, Dr. Bennett called to say that he got Nick's CT scan results. Things look good, so he feels it's okay to move ahead with placing a new implant on Nick's lower left.

Thursday, October 23, 2008

    Nick and I dropped Kenzie at my mom's this morning and headed to his appointment with Dr. Bennett. When we went in to discuss today's surgery, Dr. Bennett said that he wanted to relieve Nick's brand-new denture. That means that he would drill out some of the acrylic. I told him that I wasn't comfortable with that because it would weaken the denture. He told me that if we didn't allow him to do it, then he wouldn't do the implant surgery.

    He finally said that if Nick left the denture out for the next two months for healing, he would do the surgery. In hindsight, I wish we would have walked out.

    When the surgery was over, Dr. Bennett came out and told me that he placed two implants, but one is on a tilt so we will probably only be able to use it as a rest for the denture. That is ludicrous! Why place an implant if it can't be used properly? Because you screwed up, that's why. I am now a firm believer that implants are best placed by a periodontist and not an oral surgeon, at least not that oral surgeon.

    I understand that Nick has a unique situation, but to have one implant fail then place another incorrectly, something is not kosher. I have always been impressed at the placement of implants by the periodontist that our office refers to, I should have had Nick go there.

Friday, November 14, 2008

    I am finding that being co-chair of P.T.O fundraising is a lot more work than I expected. For the last two weeks, I have been planning out Book Fair posters, sending wish lists to teachers, planning guessing games for the kids, and figuring out decorations to fit our jungle theme. Today, I spent the day at school setting up the Book Fair,
    Now, normally I wouldn't think it was a big deal, but Kenzie only goes to kindergarten in the afternoon. This volunteer "job" takes all day. Kenzie was a fantastic help all morning, then I walked her to her class, and continued to set up.
    After school, she helped again until we left at 4:30. It was a long day for me, never mind a five-year-old.
    Next week, she will be hanging out at the book fair for the three mornings that I am not at work because I agreed to volunteer. Thank God she's a good kid!

Sunday, November 30, 2008

The Book Fair was a success, and we finished a gift card fundraiser as well. Kenzie has been enjoying my volunteering in the library and so have I.

Thanksgiving was nice, but not the same. Krista and I had a disagreement recently about the girls joining the same club, so things were a bit tense.

Krista wanted Gwen to join the club and had asked me not to let Kenzie. I felt that if Kenzie wanted to join, she should be able to. I understand that Krista wants Gwen to gain confidence without Kenzie. With us living in the same town, there is a likelihood that both girls will want to join the same clubs or do the same sports. Neither of us are wrong, but that doesn't solve the problem either.

I hate when there's a rift in our family. Nonetheless, we did still get together with my parents, aunts and uncle for dinner and Krista's family joined us for dessert.

Kenzie and I spent this weekend decorating for Christmas. I love that she enjoys it as much as I do! We did some cookie baking as well. Her favorite cookies to make are sugar cookies because she loves to get creative with the icing.

Kyle and Nick have been hunting quite a bit. My anxiety when he goes out still spikes. He has gotten a couple of bucks this week so most of the weekend he was outside butchering them. Today, I helped him package some of the burger too.

Saturday, December 6, 2008

    This week was a busy one! The P.T.O. ran the school Christmas store. I helped on the three days that I could. It was fun to help the littles shop for their families. Kenzie had a ball buying for my parents, Gloria, Gwen, Krista, John, and Nick with me. She then asked me to go out of the store so she could buy for me too.
    Today was the culmination of the Christmas Store with a Christmas Bazaar too. I spent a lot of time putting together raffle baskets at night this week as well as prepping for Breakfast with Santa this morning. Everything went well and the P.T.O raised a good amount of money to help support field trips and special guests for the kids.
    Yesterday, Nick went to my office to have his denture relieved by my boss. He had seen Dr. Bennett earlier this week and got the okay to start wearing his denture once it was relieved. Since Nick doesn't have the amount of gum tissue that most people would have, food gets stuck under the denture A LOT. I feel for him. It's like learning to chew all over again.

Friday, December 19, 2008

    Winter Storm Austin hit today. No school for Kenzie! We got over a foot of snow and it's still falling tonight.
    Gloria flew here on Tuesday, and we had so much fun playing out in the snow with her today. Of course, Nick and I were busy shoveling a lot too, but that didn't stop us from pulling Kenzie in the sled and laughing when she'd fall out.
    Gloria sat in the kitchen with me tonight while I made thirteen cookie trays for gifts. I am praying that the roads are safe tomorrow so that we can go out and deliver them.
    The four of us spent the rest of the evening watching Christmas movies together and drinking cocoa by the woodstove. The perfect end to a snowy day!

Tuesday, December 23, 2008

  This week in December continues to be a tough one for us. I can't believe it's been four years since the accident.
  Today was a very sad day for all of us. Nick's Brittany spaniel, who he has had since she was a pup, had to be put down. Nick had found blood in her food dish this morning, so he brought her to the vet. They found a large tumor in her left sinus and swelling in her brain. Putting her down was the right thing to do.
  She was an awesome dog for fourteen years. She had had glaucoma which even with eye drops could not be controlled so her eye was extracted several years ago. She adapted so amazingly too. She was the first dog that I ever felt comfortable around. I was always petrified of dogs until she warmed my heart by laying on my cold feet almost ten years ago. We are heartbroken.

Thursday, December 25, 2008, ~ Christmas

    Last night was a mellow evening with my parents, Gloria, aunts, and uncle. We had finger rolls, cold cuts, and salads for dinner, then cookies for dessert after mass.

    Kenzie enjoyed watching Santa's progress once again on the computer and couldn't wait to go to sleep. She carefully chose her cookies and carrots for Santa and the reindeer before going to bed.

    This morning, she was full of energy and excitement. She called my parents to let them know that we were awake, and they could come over. Gloria had a glimmer in her eyes watching Kenzie unwrap her gifts too.

    We all went to Krista's for an Italian Christmas dinner. John's parents, grandmother, and aunt were there too.

    Things are still not the same between Krista and me. Unfortunately, I think it's starting to affect Kenzie and Gwen too. They are both much snottier to one another. It's much better than it was, but I can see subtle differences that make me sad for our relationship as well as theirs.

Wednesday, December 31, 2008

The year is ending with a bang. Poor Nick called out sick for work. He's been vomiting since last night.

We had ten inches of snow today, so I shoveled quite a bit to keep Nick from feeling that he had to do anything.

We were supposed to have Dean, Tammy, and the kids here tonight, but between Nick being sick and the snow, they cancelled. I can't blame them.

I'm not sure if it's my hormones, or what, but Gloria has been getting on my nerves this week too. She has been asking probing questions about my issues with Krista and getting in between Nick and I too. When she's here, Nick has no opinion on anything, so I get answers like, "I don't care" or "Doesn't matter to me". Sometimes I wonder if Gloria has been acting the way she is because she's upset with what is going on back home. She alluded to a financial predicament that she was put in by another family member, and I know it's weighing on her mind. But I am so frustrated with her preoccupation here. She is here until January 8th; I just hope that she and I can enjoy the time we have left together.

Gloria went to bed at 10:45 tonight and Kenzie and I snuggled in her bed and slept a bit until her alarm went off at 11:45. We woke up Nick, turned on the TV, and brought in the New Year together.

Wednesday, February 4, 2009

After a month of sledding, ice skating, sinusitis, head colds and ridiculous amounts of snow, we flew to FLORIDA early this morning! Since it was snowing last night, and we had an early flight, we all stayed at a hotel near the airport. We landed in sunny Orlando at 9:50 am!

We took the shuttle to Disney's Pop Century Resort, checked in, and got settled in our rooms. Krista, John, and Gwen have an adjoining room to ours. My parents and John's parents also have adjoining rooms.

Since today was a travel day, we hadn't planned on going to any of the parks. Instead, we all went shopping in Downtown Disney.

We had dinner tonight at the Raglan Road Pub. It was an excellent meal, but the entertainment was what really made it awesome. They had extremely talented Irish dancers performing. It was hard to take my eyes off them long enough to take another bite of food!

Tonight, the kids went for a swim in the hotel pool then we got them to bed by eight. Tomorrow, we head to the Magic Kingdom!

Thursday, February 12, 2009

Today was our last full day at Disney. Though we will have some time here tomorrow, our bags will be in storage until we take the shuttle to the airport.

What a fantastic week it has been! I absolutely LOVE Disney and to share it with Kenzie, well, that was extra special.

While we were here, we visited all four Disney Parks. We spent three days at the Magic Kingdom. Our family's favorite rides are Pirates of the Caribbean, Big Thunder Mountain, Splash Mountain, and the Jungle Cruise. We love the Country Bear Jamboree and watching Tinkerbell's flight from Cinderella's Castle into Tomorrowland before the fireworks gave me goosebumps. We did a character breakfast/Meet and Greet too. I have to say, the Magic Kingdom has always been my favorite Disney Park, and it still is.

One day was spent at EPCOT. The girls were amazingly patient while we waited eighty minutes to ride Soarin'. It was very cool and worth the wait! Kenzie loved The Land and all the vertically growing vegetables too. I liked going through each of the countries as well. Our lunch that day was a side trip to the Wilderness Lodge's Whispering Pines café. Yum!

We went to Disney's Hollywood Studios on two occasions. Kenzie shocked us by riding the Tower of Terror with my mom and Nick. She was very disappointed that she wasn't tall enough for the Rock-n-Roller Coaster though. Gwen was tall enough, and teased Kenzie a bit about that. Well, that came back and bit Gwen in the buns because that ride scared the heck out of her.

The poor kid was screaming and crying at the top of her lungs, and when the ride finally stopped, Krista literally had to pry her fingers from the grab bar just to get her off the ride. One day while we were there, we did a side trip for dinner at the Grand Floridian too. What an excellent meal!

The safari ride at Animal Kingdom was fantastic, as was the Tusker House buffet. The Tree of Life was astonishing, and the Bug's Life show inside it had the kids giggling at the feeling of "bugs" wiggling under their bottoms. Kenzie was tall enough to ride the Everest rollercoaster, and she loved it. She's our little daredevil for sure!

On the warmest day of the trip, we all went to Blizzard Beach. Kenzie did some of the bigger water slides with us, but most of the day was spent in the Pre-teen area just swimming and doing the zipline into the pool. We went to the Polynesian Resort's O'Hana for a family style dinner that night. After dinner, the staff taught all the kids a Hawaiian dance. Nick and John were fantastic sports when they were asked to put on grass skirts and hold the limbo stick for the kids. The girls loved that their daddies did that!

Most days we swam at some point in the day. There were many buffet breakfasts at the resort, and I can say without a doubt that no one was ever hungry on this trip! I hate the thought of going home tomorrow.

Tuesday, March 24, 2009

Since we've been home from Disney, things have been very busy. With Krista and I still watching each other's kid, and the girls in kindergarten, Gwen in the morning and Kenzie in the afternoon, the running around is endless.

Nick has spoken to two different police departments about the accident. I went to his first presentation and wanted to cry when he got choked up talking about it. He did very well though and I was extremely proud of him.

Work has been busy and the P.T.O. fundraisers are non-stop. My time in the school Library is still a lot of fun and it has already been hinted to me that I am welcome to do it again next year.

Nick has been drinking more and I hate it. I don't like how he acts when he's had too much to drink, and his total disregard for my feelings has caused some stress in our relationship. Cary is dealing with much the same at her house, except Brandon does it a lot more often than Nick. I wish that the two of them would realize that drinking is not a coping mechanism.

Sometimes it seems like my world is out of control. Today, I did something I am not proud of, but man did it feel right when I was doing it.

I picked up Kenzie at school this afternoon, and as I turned the corner toward our driveway, I saw two kids on a four-wheeler flying down our private dirt road. I flew down the road behind them and laid on my horn. When they finally stopped, I yelled at them and told them that they didn't belong down there and had been told to stay out before. The next time I saw them, I would call the police.

It was then that I saw my neighbor working on the road in his New Holland tractor. He gave me a thumbs up, but I'm sure he was thinking "what a nut job".

I also realized that Kenzie had been yelling, "Woo Hoo! Faster Mommy, faster!", as I sped down the dirt road, hitting potholes and rocks alike. I definitely did not win the mother of the year award today, but I did give my kid one heck of a fun ride.

I am really looking forward to blowing off some steam on Saturday with Cary. She and I are heading to the casino for dinner, shopping, and a little gambling on the slots. More than anything, we need our time to chat, just us, and no one else.

On Sunday, Nick is starting his training as a Hunter Safety Course Instructor. It's something that he has been thinking about for a while, and I think his story might make new hunters think before they shoot.

Friday, April 24, 2009

  Easter was full of tradition with our egg hunts and breakfast buffet at the casino with the family. Kenzie got a jewelry armoire with earrings from the Easter Bunny since she recently got her ears pierced.
  Fishing and camping seasons are underway too. We have already spent several evenings on the jon boat fishing for crappie, and a weekend in the camper.
  The school Book Fair ended today. I have spent three days helping there, as well as my Library time and an extra hour in Kenzie's class teaching the kids about dental health.
  I felt honored when the school principal asked me to be on the hiring team for a new school psychologist too. Kenzie's principal is a very kindhearted man and I respect him immensely. He has no problem doing silly things, like shaving his mustache off on the school tv station, as a reward for the goals he sets for the student body. So, when he asked for my help, I quickly accepted.
  We have been talking about visiting Nick's family, so I have been checking airline ticket prices for the last two weeks. Unfortunately, his family keeps going back and forth on when the timing will work, so now the prices have doubled, and he decided that we aren't going. Though I am bummed about not going, I am relieved that a decision has finally been made and I can stop watching the prices.

Wednesday, April 29, 2009

Krista and I chaperoned the kindergarten field trip to the zoo today. Each of us had our own child and a classmate. Both of us "lucked out" with an extremely busy child that didn't listen. It was a day that called for a lot of patience! In the end, we did have fun though.

My boss called me on my cell phone while I was at the zoo. He asked me to make a list of every surgery that Nick has had as well as the date of each surgery. Apparently, our insurance does not want to pay for Nick's denture because it is considered to have been too long of a period of time between the accident and the fabrication of the denture. Do they think that he would wait to get a denture if he could have gotten one sooner? Do they think that he wouldn't want to have an easier time eating? How was he supposed to keep it in his mouth without the implants? It's all so exasperating!

When I got home, I went back through my records (thank God that I'm anal) and typed up the list for him. I emailed it out tonight. I appreciate that he is writing a letter to our insurance company and including as much information as possible. I just hope he can get them to pay for it.

Saturday, May 2, 2009

    Kenzie had her second soccer game today. So far, she seems to like it! Her team lost 3-1 but she didn't mind at all. She just likes playing. The team made a big circle around Kenzie after the game and sang "Happy Birthday" to her as well!
    After the game, we got her changed in the car and headed to Dinosaur Ridge Park for some birthday fun. She panned for pyrite and unearthed fossils among other activities there. Since it was her birthday, the staff really made a big deal of her, and she had a blast.
    When we got home, my parents, Krista, John, Gwen, and our neighbors came over for cupcakes and ice cream. Once again, our little girl was treated to beautiful gifts, well wishes, and phone calls from Melanie, Gloria, Geena and Cary. This is the first time that Gloria isn't here for Kenzie's birthday in a few years. She's having surgery next week though, so she needed to stay close to home.
    Next Saturday, we're having a party for Kenzie with her school friends at the Town Hall pool. She chose a "Little Mermaid" theme for this year. She's one lucky kid!

Tuesday, June 23, 2009

The last month or so has been filled with soccer games, camping, work, and fun. It feels like I have been on an emotional roller coaster.

Nick has been very easy to irritate lately. Once he's frustrated, he rants. When we were camping recently, and Kenzie saw him crabbing at me, she tried to intervene. She picked some wildflowers from the safari field at the campground and handed them to Nick. I overheard her tell him, "Plan two Daddy, give these to Mommy. I want to help you guys keep loving each other." I was between wanting to melt at her thoughtfulness and feeling horrible that she would think that we wouldn't love each other.

My first-year volunteering in the school Library ended last week. I now know how to use the computer system to check out books and have even covered for the librarian one day while she attended a funeral. We have already established that I will be back in the fall.

The P.T.O. had a very productive school year with several fundraisers, two book fairs, and a field day yesterday. I helped with each activity and ran a station at field day too.

Today was Kenzie's last day of kindergarten. She had a great report card and is excited that she will have some of her friends in her class in the fall.

I am excited to get our summer together started. Although Kenzie told me that she hated me for the first-time last week, we mended the fence quickly and she apologized. Most parents that I speak to dread having their kids home all summer. I can't wait!

Sunday, August 9, 2009

This weekend we went on a camping trip, and it was much needed. It was good to get away and think of something else, when the last several weeks have had me continuously worried.

Kenzie has had body aches and pains for several months. We discussed it with her pediatrician at her six-year-old physical, but he wasn't overly concerned about it. Her discomfort kept getting worse, so I called in the beginning of July to ask him to check her again. He had us take her for bloodwork, and it showed that she had elevated anti-nuclear antibodies. Her pediatrician called me at work to tell me that she may have rheumatoid arthritis, and like any other neurotic mother, I burst into tears when I got off the phone.

Fast forward to last week, we saw a rheumatologist at Harris Children's Hospital, and he feels that Kenzie's level is so low, that it is nothing to worry about. Yet, I spent an entire month worrying until we had the appointment. Go figure.

My female issues have gotten so much worse, my gynecologist is now recommending a hot water endometrial ablation. They basically will use hot water to burn out the sloughing cells in my uterus. I have to say, I am NOT looking forward to it, but if it makes life more manageable and less painful, I am all for it.

Nick flew back to his childhood home for a family reunion last month. It was the first time that Kenzie and I have not gone with him. I am glad he went but hated not being together. We have had a rough time lately. He is very impatient and short tempered. Between his injuries and my lady issues, our personal life is not what either of us want and coping with that has been difficult.

Monday, August 31, 2009

Today was Kenzie's first day of First Grade! She has been so excited for school to start.

Krista called this morning and asked if we could follow each other to school and walk the girls in together. Gwen was feeling a bit timid.

We walked them in, and their teacher, Mrs. McConnell, had an excited welcome for them. The energy that she has is contagious! I think this is going to be an awesome year!

When Kenzie got home, she told me all about her day. Krista and Gwen came over for forty-five minutes too, and it was obvious that Gwen likes Mrs. McConnell too.

Kenzie had requested pancakes and bacon for supper today and she scarfed them right down. After supper, we put on our pajamas, snuggled, and talked.

Nick spent the evening in the garage working on a set of Adirondack chairs for Kyle. Kyle came over to help too. He never even came in to tuck Kenzie in with me. I'm disappointed in him. He had come home with flowers for her, which was very thoughtful, but she would have preferred his time. She told me, "Mommy, I'm sad that Daddy isn't snuggling too."

I know he does a lot with Kenzie, but because of that, when it doesn't happen, it is surely missed. I'm sure he didn't even think of it. He's been working hard to finish Kyle's chairs. He is so grateful for everything Kyle has done for us since the accident, it's a small way to feel like he's helping Kyle too.

Wednesday, September 30, 2009

This month is a total blur. On Labor Day, we celebrated my aunt and uncle's 50th wedding anniversary. They had a large group at our local VFW, and it was a very nice day.

On the very next day, my uncle's sister passed away unexpectedly. She has spent every holiday with our family since I was a child. I miss her dearly.

Kenzie started taking gymnastics classes and Gwen started horseback lessons. Gwen continues to give Krista a horrible time about riding the bus. The poor kid is just petrified to do it and that makes every morning a nightmare.

On the 5th, after I had done a ton of research, we decided to install a fiberglass in ground pool. We decided to put it in an area, close to the house, where I had previously built a large, raised bed garden with a stone retaining wall around it. The thought of taking that thirty-foot-long garden down broke my heart because I had spent weeks making it, but I have always wanted a swimming pool.

Once the decision was made, I got busy getting all the proper permits, insurance, etc. I ordered the pool online, hired a local company to install it, and ordered the pool water and winter cover. I met with stamped concrete companies and fence companies too, then hired the one that I felt comfortable with. In the matter of twenty-five days, we now have an in-ground pool!

It was delivered today on the back of a flat-bed truck and the guys who installed it just lifted it with their excavator on a "sling" and set it in place. While the pool water was pumped into the pool, the contractors and I pushed sand under it and around it. We had to fill in the outside at the same rate as the inside to prevent the walls from warping. When all was said and done, we did a pretty good job.

When Kenzie got home from school today, she threw on her Ariel swimsuit and jumped into the fifty-degree water. She swam from one end to the other and jumped out. Her lips were already purple, and she was shaking like a leaf, but she got in her swim!

Monday, October 5, 2009

Nick started his new position as a second shift lieutenant at the Barnard Correctional Facility today. He will be on second shift for one week for training, then third shift after that. Though I am not excited about his new hours, I am excited that he is now working eight miles from home instead of forty plus. He will now have inmate interaction again, but the inmates housed there are either end of sentence or non-violent crimes for the most part.

The pool contractors had a rough time getting their excavator out of our yard and accidentally destroyed our underground electric to the garage last week. The electrician came out to fix that the next day so no harm no foul.

The contractors also poured hundreds of gallons of water where the pool deck was going and rolled the soil for an entire day in preparation for the cement patio. They set up the forms on Friday, and when I came home today, I had a beautiful stamped concrete pool deck and a working pool.

Now we just need to get the fence contractor here and Nick and I need to complete the stone retaining wall between the house and the pool. I can't believe how well this is coming along!

Tuesday, October 13, 2009

Nolan, Gina, and Eliza came to visit from last Thursday until today. We made the most of our short time with them!

On Friday, Gina and I went into Boston to shop and hit the famous tourist spots. She encouraged me to get a new haircut, so we went to a salon there. It cost me seventy dollars for the cut and blow-dry. I almost keeled over when I was told the price.

Nick, Nolan, and Eliza worked on the retaining wall until Kenzie got out of school, then the three of them took our camper and met us at a campground just north of the city. After two hours in the camper, the seventy-dollar haircut still hadn't been noticed by anyone.

On Saturday, we all went to Salem. Geena had always wanted to see Salem, especially at Halloween time, and we had a really good time. The whole town and museums are very eerie and boy, did we see some interesting people!

We spent Sunday and Monday at home, working on the wall, playing the Wii, and having fun with the kids. The girls got along very well. I couldn't believe the amount of hugs and kisses they bestowed on each other this week!

Today, Nick brought Nolan, Geena, and Eliza to the airport. It was a tearful goodbye as usual. I hated to see them go. The pool fence was installed today too, and it looks fantastic!

Tonight, Nick started third shift. I am a wreck about trying to keep Kenzie and Gwen quiet while he sleeps from now on. He has reassured me that he'll be fine, but I know if it's not quiet, he won't get the rest he needs.

Saturday, October 24, 2009

No rest for the weary.

Yesterday I had my endometrial ablation. I was a nervous wreck before I got to the hospital. Kenzie had put a little note in my pocket before I went, wishing me well and telling me that she loves me. She's such a sweetheart. All went well. I had minimal discomfort and was told to relax for the weekend.

This morning, Kenzie woke us up by running through our bedroom AS she was vomiting. Nick stayed in bed, and I got up to wash the floor and tend to her. The poor kid vomited multiple times today. I was very sore, but she was inhabiting the couch, so I went outside to shovel stone under the pool fence. Not my brightest idea, nor was covering the swimming pool with the help of my parents. I am hurting tonight and have an alarming amount of bleeding. Time to just lay here and relax.

Tuesday, November 17, 2009

Today is Gloria's 75th birthday! The three of us called to wish her a happy birthday and tell her how much we miss her. They still haven't figured out what is causing her stomach issues, so she had to cancel her fall trip here.

It's Book Fair time again and I am helping. I relinquished my co-chair of fundraising position at the beginning of the school year, but I am still just as involved. I made and set up the Teacher Wish List board and I worked the register today. I will be helping on Thursday and Friday as well. Kenzie came to get her books today and was very excited to have me shop with her.

Nick and I went to "Lunch with Someone Grand" with Kenzie at the school cafeteria. He's working third shirt tonight and first shift tomorrow. He's doing the same thing tomorrow night, so he is going to be exhausted.

Kenzie has been giving me a hard time about going to school for the last couple of weeks. She says it's because she'll miss me, but I wonder if there's something else going on. She loves Mrs. McConnell, so I know it's not that. I am one of the room moms, so I am there frequently. She seems happy there.

I am helping in the Library every Thursday this school year. I love that my friend, Erica, isn't just acting as a librarian, she is a teacher, and the kids are learning things. I am learning too!

After thirty-four years in the plumbing and heating business, my dad has decided to close his business. Due to a screwed up spinal stenosis surgery, he is no longer able to lift his arms and do his job. This is going to be a major change in his and Mom's life.

Sunday, November 29, 2009

The last week has been a good one for the most part. Last Saturday, Cary and I took the kids to the Children's Museum. It was so much fun to watch Elizabeth and Kenzie pretend. They both have awesome imaginations and play very well together.

We all celebrated my parents' 42nd wedding anniversary on the twenty third, and Nick had time to get some hunting in, so he was happy.

Gwen was sick so she stayed home from school, but she was better in time for our Thanksgiving dinner on Thursday. We all had a great time playing the Wii after dinner, so everyone stayed later than usual and that completely made my day. Kenzie and I even had time to watch the parade that morning too!

Friday and Saturday were spent decorating for Christmas. Kenzie enjoys it more every year and I love singing carols with her as we decorate.

Tonight, the three of us, Krista, Gwen, John, and my parents all went to the Christmas Light Parade. We packed hot cocoa and needed our long johns because it was freezing out, but we had a great time.

The only downfall to this week was the unfortunate reality that my endometrial ablation did not work. In fact, things are worse now than before I had it done. I have a call in to my gynecologist, but with the holiday, I haven't heard back yet.

Nick has been very helpful with Kenzie this week. We are all trying to get used to his new schedule and making everything work.

Sunday, December 20, 2009, ~ Five Years Since the Accident

    Though this day haunts all of us every year, it has gotten better since Nick has gotten better. Like that day five years ago, we had snow today. But today the day was spent with family, sledding down the new path that Nick, Kenzie, and I cleared in the woods.

    My parents, Krista, John, and Gwen joined us, and we all had a blast going down the hill. Later, the kids and my parents made secret Christmas gifts for Krista and me in the basement. When Kenzie came upstairs, she said, "Mom, it's like Gwen, Mema, Poppy, and I were elves filling Santa's shelves!" That kid cracks me up!

    Tonight, when Nick and I were tucking her in, Kenzie was very anxious. She was nervous about her pajama choice for *Polar Express* Day at school tomorrow. She felt like she would be picked on. So, we got her back out of bed and revised the plan. Hopefully she sleeps well tonight.

Friday, December 25, 2009

Kenzie came running in to our room at 6:40 am. She was so excited and couldn't wait to see what Santa brought.

She loved her karaoke machine, stuffed hippo, and kid sized guitar! Mom and Dad came over to see what Santa brought and we all played the Wii Fit too.

We all went to Krista and John's for an Italian dinner. There were fourteen of us at their table. Everyone chatted and it was a very nice time.

When we got home, we called Melanie, Nolan, and Gloria. Kenzie serenaded them with her guitar. God bless their ears!

The three of us played the Wii until 8:30 pm, had a snack, and snuggled. It was a really nice day except that Nick never acts happy. He grumbles and gets angry so quickly. I thought it would get better when he healed, but instead it's getting worse. I'm so frustrated.

Sometimes I wonder if it's the reality that he now knows the difficulties that he will most likely have for the rest of his life. Maybe he had more hope before. I really don't know because he says he's fine, but his demeanor tells me otherwise. I just want him to be happy and enjoy the life we have!

The New Year is just a week away. We will usher it in with Dean, Tammy, and the kids. Nick has to work, so he will leave us before midnight. 2009 has been a good year all in all, but here's to an even better 2010!

Thursday, February 11, 2010

We have had an interesting start to the new year so far. My parents left for Florida right after the first and are enjoying the warmth and sunshine. They drive their motorhome down and travel from one campground to the next, until the spirit (and warmer temperatures here) moves them to come home.

Kenzie had her first research project for school. It was on harbor seals, and she loved learning about them. She is enjoying gymnastics, and we have taken her to the ice rink and roller rink as well.

Nick had a checkup with Dr. Bennett last month and he told him that things are looking better than ever! His job is going well so far.

Last week, Kenzie woke up with two red and crusty eyes. A trip to the pediatrician confirmed pink eye, so no school for her for a couple of days.

I had a checkup with my gynecologist. Since things have gotten worse since the endometrial ablation, he feels that a partial hysterectomy is needed. Now my goal is to get the house in order and do my spring cleaning before he schedules me for surgery. I know I can't continue to live the way that I have been, so it needs to be done. He feels that the progesterone shots for invitro are to blame. My body remembers wanting to build a soft layer of cells much like a computer would have an image "burned" into the screen if it weren't for a screensaver.

This morning, Kenzie woke up with earaches, so back to the pediatrician we went. She has a double ear infection, so our plans for the indoor water park this weekend have been rescheduled.

Tuesday, February 23, 2010

    Yesterday, Nick was eating soup for supper, and he jumped up quickly and ran to the bathroom. He had heard a crunching noise and went to look in the mirror. He told me that he felt like something shifted in his jaw. He immediately called Dr. Bennett.

    This morning, Nick went to see Dr. Bennett. Dr. Bennett took a Panorex x-ray and confirmed that the reconstruction plate is broken (a diagonal break) on left side. He said he has never seen this happen, so he needs to make some calls and get back to us.

    Nick is scared, and so am I. What happened to "it looks better than it ever has?" I thought titanium was supposed to be strong. Don't they make golf clubs out of it?

    When I was spring cleaning our half bath, I just sat down on the floor and cried. Nick doesn't need to see me this upset, he has enough on his mind. He's back to only soft foods. I hope that Dr. Bennett can figure out what to do.

    As if all of this wasn't enough, Kenzie woke up vomiting this morning. She couldn't keep anything down. I set her up on the couch-bed in the sunroom and she napped. When she woke up, she was shaking uncontrollably and couldn't even hold the thermometer in her mouth. She wasn't totally coherent either. She had 101.6 fever and could not keep Tylenol down. We called the pediatrician and he recommended that we bring her to the Emergency Room. We did, and they gave her Zofran under her tongue, a strep test and sent us home.

Thursday, February 25, 2010

Kenzie is still sick but not vomiting. She's very weak and dizzy, but I think she is on the mend.

Dr. Bennett called this morning and recommended removing the loose portions of reconstruction plate, leaving only 2 sections with screws in place. He is unsure if bone is broken and due to the amount of metal in Nick's mouth, there would be too many artifacts on a CT scan for him to be able to see for sure. He will evaluate the bone in the Operating Room to decide if a bone graft from Nick's hip is needed. He is also uncertain if the bone that he placed during the last surgery will withstand long term without a reconstruction plate. He feels that it will be OK for now. He told me, "You'll never be done with this."

I got off the phone and cried. My poor husband is in for a lifetime of this crap. It breaks my heart. We had finally gotten to a point where we could eat a meal together without the stress of feeling that I was eating too fast and would be done long before he was. For the longest time, he wouldn't eat his whole meal because it took him too long and he would get frustrated.

He can't feel his lower lip, so he doesn't know when he dribbles out food. When we tell him, or he sees it on the table in front of him, it pisses him off. How could it not? He's a grown man made to feel like he's learning to eat all over again. And now, that struggle will resurface once again as he learns to deal with whatever this next surgery brings. He chokes frequently now due to the scar tissue and malformation. More surgeries mean more scar tissue and more trouble with eating. I am heartbroken for him.

Once I got my head wrapped around this mess, I went online and did yet another search for specialists. I called one about 4 hours from us and left a message. They called me back this afternoon and gave Nick an appointment for next week.

Wednesday, March 3, 2010

    I took today off, and Nick and I drove four hours from home last night. We stayed at a hotel near the hospital where he was to have another second opinion. I had photocopied his two hundred-plus page medical record, so the specialist could review that as well as the photo album of his surgeries. Kenzie slept at Krista's house last night.
    All of that for a fifteen-minute meet and greet with Dr. Felix where he told us that Dr. Bennett has done fine. He might have done the free fibular graft if he had done it, but everything that was done is fine.
    We are totally exasperated! We need someone to have a fresh idea to fix Nick!
    Nick and I picked Kenzie up after school, and the three of us called Eliza to wish her a happy birthday. They are going to be celebrating out there, so we will be enjoying some pictures soon.
    A medical assistant for Dr. Mallon, the orthopedic surgeon for Nick's shin cyst, called today. She wants Nick to go in to be evaluated for intubation for his cyst removal surgery. For the life of us, we have no idea why he would need to be intubated to remove a cyst from his shin. I asked her to please speak to Dr. Mallon and have him speak to Dr. Bennett as well.
    Dr. Mallon called Nick tonight. Dr. Bennett has not returned his calls, but he will do an epidural for surgery since he cannot intubate orally.

Tuesday, March 9, 2010

My mom got Kenzie on the bus for us this morning so Nick and I could go to his surgery appointment with Dr. Mallon for 8am. They took him in for surgery at 9:15, and he was in recovery by 10:05. All went well. He is to stay off his leg for a couple of days. He didn't get the feeling back in his legs until after 2pm.

When we got home, Mom and Dad were here with Kenzie. She helped me set up the couch bed for Nick so that he wouldn't need to go upstairs.

I called Dr. Bennett's office to see if they had an appointment for Nick's surgery. We have been waiting for Dr. Bennett to call with a date since February 25th. The receptionist told me that he is out of the office for the rest of the week. This is ridiculous!

At supper time, Kenzie was so proud because she made her daddy's puree all by herself! She went upstairs and got his toothbrush and pajamas too. I love that she likes to be a little helper!

Cary called tonight. She has checked on us frequently, especially knowing that Nick is broken again. I love that I have a friend that I can tell anything to. She is beyond understanding. When Nick's titanium plate broke last month, I told Cary that I can't call her house. I will call her cell phone if I want to reach her, but I can't talk to Brandon. He has made no effort to be involved and check on Nick. He is the last person that I want to speak to.

Sunday, March 21, 2010

Gwen and Kenzie have been so cute together this week. Kenzie invited Gwen here for "Scarf Club" and they played with scarves, and I made scarf shaped grilled cheese sandwiches for lunch. The next day, Gwen invited Kenzie to her house for "Hat Club". I love when they play so well together!

Tonight, we went to my parents' house for Sunday dinner. All was going well, and we had a nice time, until Mom told me that she needs to know our surgery schedule because she has things she wants to do with Senior Citizens. Though I understand that she wants to make plans, she also knows my frustration with the fact that both Nick and I are in the need of surgery and neither of our doctors have committed to a date yet. She knows that I am having a lot of anxiety because my hysterectomy may cause me to need some help and I need to be able to help Nick after his surgery. I have no idea if I will be able to bend to do his post-surgical care if my surgery is first.

I know that she doesn't need to be here to help, that's not her job. We are adults and should be able to take care of this ourselves. But we have always been there for each other. The thought that now I'm not going to feel comfortable asking for help because I will feel like it's an imposition, has me wanting to sit and cry.

Nick's blood sugars have been all over the place since his titanium plate broke. He has had to increase his insulin multiple times. I can't wait for him to have his surgery.

Tuesday, March 30, 2010

Kenzie was very upset last night and told me that she was scared. She said, "I don't want you to go to the hospital!" I told her, "I'll be fine. I need to be so that I can come home to the little girl that I love more than anything in the world."

This morning, she snuggled with me before Nick and I dropped her off to John and headed to the hospital for my hysterectomy. She wished me luck.

My surgery only took about fifty minutes. They gave me a spinal and IV sedation. I woke up feeling pretty good.

If all goes well, I will head home in the morning. I called Kenzie tonight to say goodnight. They haven't found a room for me yet so I may be spending the night in recovery.

Monday, April 5, 2010

My recovery is slow going. Yesterday, I woke up in a lot of pain, doubled over actually. I took Motrin and went back to bed. Thankfully, Kenzie was very patient about going downstairs to see what the Easter Bunny brought.

Krista and John were great and had Easter brunch at their house this year so I wouldn't have to go out. We had French toast, bacon, sausage, eggs, muffins, and beverages. It was a relaxing day.

Mom and Dad picked me up this morning to go grocery shopping. My legs got so weak while I was walking through the store, I thought I was going to collapse. Nick was at home when we got here, so he carried in the bags and put the groceries away for me.

This afternoon, Nick had his pre-op appointment with Dr. Bennett. Dr. Bennett took a new x-ray and told Nick that the broken ends to the reconstruction plate now overlap each other by one-half inch. There is no doubt that the bone is broken. Nick will need bilateral posterior hip bone grafts and new reconstruction plates. Dr. Bennett also told Nick that he is going on a two week vacation the week after Nick's surgery, so his resident will follow Nick and remove the sutures.

I can't help but wonder, if Dr. Bennett had addressed the broken reconstruction plate right away, would Nick still have broken bone? Unfortunately, we will never know.

Gwen has bilateral pneumonia. Krista needs to "pound" on her back to loosen the mucus. The poor kid is miserable!

Tuesday, April 13, 2010

Nick and I picked Dad up at 3am to go to Harris Hospital. Kenzie had slept at their house last night so we wouldn't have to wake her this morning.

I went to Pre-Op with Nick and was made very anxious by the Anesthesiologist who gave a nervous laugh in between everything he did. The nurse who was helping said, "We'll do an IV next, and it's going to hurt." You have to love (feel the sarcasm) these health care providers who have no clue how to speak to their patients.

Nick went into surgery at 7:50 am, and Dr. Bennett came out to speak to me at 2:10pm. He told me that everything went well. The reconstruction plate was broken on the bottom left. He took bone from Nick's right posterior hip and placed it in the broken area, then placed a new titanium plate. He didn't need to harvest bone from the left hip like he had thought.

Dad and I visited with Nick in recovery for a while, then went to Mom and Dad's. Mom had picked Gloria up at the airport with Kenzie, and I was so happy to see her!

Gloria, Kenzie, and I came home and got Gloria settled in. Kenzie and I showed her the pool too. Nick had opened it last week and had put out the pool furniture so we can recover from our surgeries out there. Gloria loved it!

Friday, April 16, 2010

    Gloria and I visited Nick on Wednesday. He was swollen and sore but doing okay. Dr. Bennett released him from the hospital at 1:30, so we got him home and settled in.

    Kenzie is keeping Gloria quite busy. She loves having her Nanny here and now that she has homework, she wants Nanny's help. Her favorite homework is Mrs. McConnell's spelling work. She is given multiple options on what she can do for homework and must pick three to do. Her favorite is to write her spelling words in shaving cream on the countertop. I must admit, I really like that one too.

    Gloria, Nick, and I dropped Kenzie off at school and went to Dr. Bennett's this morning. Dr. Bennett had me remove part of Nick's 10" x 15" bandage, then he removed the rest. He also removed the local IV from Nick's hip. Nick can now eat soft foods, and starting tomorrow, we should use half strength peroxide in his mouth.

    Nick's endocrinologist has changed his insulin to help after surgery. So far it seems to be helping.

    The four of us watched a movie together and relaxed tonight. It's been a whirlwind of a week.

Monday, April 19, 2010

Nick had a few rough days between pain and dry heaving over the weekend. He was much better today.

He and I realized that we have an issue with the air intake on the pool, so we attempted to figure it out. I'm not quite sure if we got it fixed, but we'll see.

Tonight, Kenzie "surprised" us with a "date" in the living room. She and Gloria put a table and chairs in the middle of the floor and set the table complete with candlelight and daffodils.

Kenzie had made menus for us and acted like a waitress. Nick ordered a pureed peanut butter and banana sandwich, and I had a salad and cookies.

She took our photo with the camera that the Easter Bunny brought her, then returned with a bill for $20. Nick gave her a $2 tip and Kenzie ran into the kitchen and we heard her tell Gloria, "I can't believe they're really going to pay me!" She was so excited and giggled as she spoke. It was such a sweet idea and turned out to be fun! It's little moments like those that you never forget.

Friday, April 30, 2010

We've had another busy week! As usual, we are on a roller coaster of emotions too.

On Tuesday, I had a checkup with my gynecologist. I am not healing properly. He told me to be sure that I don't lift anything and to take it easy. That meant telling my boss that I needed to extend my time off for another two weeks according to my doctor.

On Wednesday, the four of us went fishing and relaxed. Kyle and some of Nick's other friends were there too. We had fun bantering between the boats on the pond.

Thursday was Kenzie's first grade class trip to the aquarium. Krista and I each had one child plus our own to watch. It was a very fun day! We saw the sea lion show and had a picnic lunch too.

Poor Kenzie was walking and trying to zip her sweatshirt at the same time. She walked headfirst into a metal pole and knocked herself to the ground. You could tell she had no clue what had happened. I was very impressed that she didn't cry, she hit her head pretty hard.

Today, I had surgery on my big toe. They removed the whole right side of the nail and nail bed. You just can't make this stuff up. There is ALWAYS something going on!

Brandon came over today for the first time since we installed the wood boiler four years ago. He gave Nick a copy of the full police report. He had very little to say and left quickly.

Nick spent quite a bit of time reading the report tonight. Since Brandon still won't talk, there are still so many unanswered questions.

Saturday, May 1, 2010

    Kenzie woke up early, very excited for her annual birthday trip to the zoo. Nick, Gloria, and I followed her lead as she took us to each animal enclosure and told us facts too. Kenzie even managed to talk Gloria into riding Mumbai the elephant with us! Later, I talked Gloria into going on the Sky Ride too! I give Gloria credit; she steps out of her comfort zone frequently when she is with us. I love sharing these experiences with her!

    When we got home, my parents, Krista, Gwen, John, and my aunt came for cake and ice cream for Kenzie's birthday. Cary and the girls called to sing the *Happy Birthday* song to Kenzie over the phone too. Geena and Melanie called her as well. I think Kenzie had a great birthday!

    I am getting very frustrated with Dr. Bennett. The last couple of times that I went with Nick for appointments, I have mentioned that Nick stops breathing multiple times every night. I mentioned it last year too. Dr. Bennett refuses to believe that Nick's tongue is sliding back and stopping his breathing. This never happened before the accident. Nick is thin and doesn't have any of the other precursors to sleep apnea, so to me, it just makes sense that it could be his tongue. All I know is, I wake up frequently and listen for him to start breathing again. If he takes more than a couple of seconds, I nudge him gently. Neither of us is getting the sleep we need.

Monday, May 31, 2010, ~ Memorial Day

After Gloria left on the 4th, we spent a lot of time setting up the blueberry patch. We had transplanted my blueberry bushes to an area near the wood line when we took down the raised bed garden to put in the pool. Since it won't be long before the blossoms turn into berries, we needed to build a surround and put up a net.

Nick offered to make a nice split rail fence around the bushes then to add posts for the net. It took him a few weeks, but it looks awesome! I special ordered the blueberry net. It's so heavy, it took four of us to cover the surround.

Dr. Bennett saw Nick for an appointment last week. He said that things look good, but he won't feel safe until six months pass. He also told Nick to go ahead and have his physician schedule a sleep study. Finally!

Kenzie continues to love gymnastics and has been invited to participate in their June Show. She is very excited!

Cary and I took the girls to a Dolly & Me Tea Party the other day. We had a good time, and I am excited to have them over for pizza and a swim in a couple weeks. That will give Cary and I a chance to visit too.

This weekend, we spent a lot of time enjoying the pool. Kenzie and I have eaten breakfast, lunch, and dinner out there for the past three days. We sat in the sun and read a bit, but most of the time we swam and played games in the pool. This has been the most relaxing weekend that we have had in quite a while, and I have thoroughly enjoyed it!

Tuesday, June 22, 2010

You just can't make this stuff up! Nick woke me up at 4:20 am with a jolt. He realized that a bat was flying around in our bedroom! Being the brave person that I am, I hid under the covers. Nick shut the bedroom door to keep it in, and it eventually flew into our bathroom. He shut that door then grabbed a net from the garage and caught it in the net. I handed him a pillowcase through the barely cracked open bathroom door and he put the bat and net in it. He went outside and released the bat.

When Kenzie heard the ruckus, she came running in all excited, and not the type of excited that her mother was! She wanted to see the bat up close. I told her I couldn't believe she wanted to go near it, and she said, "Well, I can't change my path…God gave me a path to love people and animals, and I just have to follow it." I don't know where this kid pulls this stuff from, but I love it!

I spent some time looking for the way that the bat came in and didn't have any luck. Once I got Gwen and Kenzie on the bus, I ran errands and walked the track in town with my neighbor.

Tonight, while Kenzie and I were snuggling, she said, "I learned a new word today." She pointed to her fingernail and said, "Mrs. McConnell said that my uterus is peeling." Though I wanted to die laughing, I explained to her that that was her cuticle. Of course, then she asked what her uterus is!

Sunday, July 25, 2010

Nick, Kenzie, and I finally had a real vacation together! Though we were only four hours from home, Lake Guiness was the perfect five-day getaway. I rented us a hotel room directly on the lake and the view was fantastic!

We were right in town so with the exception of going to the zoo on Thursday and the shopping outlets on Friday, everything was within walking distance. If it had not been for the rain on Friday, I would have never considered shopping, but things being as they were, why not get some Christmas gifts?

On Saturday, Kenzie begged to go parasailing. I was dead set against it because I am petrified of heights, but just like Gloria, Kenzie swayed me. I am so happy that she did too! The three of us went up together. We were strapped in, which part of me thought "this is safe" while the other part of me thought "if we go in the water, we are strapped to the parachute which will be a nice big anchor, dragging us to our deaths." Okay, I guess I was a bit dramatic in my head, but fear is fear.

The best part of parasailing was getting beyond the sound of the boat motor and hearing only the wind and the birds. It was so peaceful up there. The view was astounding over the blue water that reflected the sun and the few white clouds in the sky. For something I was sincerely against, I would definitely do it again.

Last night, we walked to the town park and listened to acoustic music. It was a perfect day before we came home today.

Monday, August 30, 2010

Summer vacation ended with a visit from Nolan, Geena, Eliza then a visit from our Florida friends. It was good to see them, but I am exhausted.

Our visit with Nolan and Geena was spent swimming and playing the Wii. Geena had a terrible head cold, so she spent their time here mostly laying by the pool and reading. I occupied Eliza and Kenzie with swimming and crafts in between cooking meals and doing laundry. With Geena feeling lousy, she went to bed early every night so she missed out on our Wii fun at night too.

I wish we had had more time between the visits and school, but our Florida friends left yesterday, and Kenzie started second grade today. She wasn't ready to get back to reality just yet and sobbed when I walked her into school. We went into the girls' room to get her put together, then I walked her to class. I felt horrible leaving her, but I knew that Mrs. Dickens would take good care of her. We had seen Mrs. Dickens on Friday night at our local fair, and she made a point of coming over to chat with Kenzie. That was so sweet of her!

When I picked Gwen and Kenzie up at school this afternoon, she had had a good day. She and Gwen swam and played together after telling me about their day. Kenzie is unsure about tomorrow and riding the bus, but she is better now than she was this morning.

My friend Erica, in the library, has already reached out for help. I will be starting next week. I enjoy being around the kids, and I like chatting with Erica too.

Friday, December 31, 2010

I can't believe this year is over already! Kenzie has grown so much, no longer has a little girl look. It makes me sad, yet I marvel at the way she expresses herself now. She's a little adult! I'm a little concerned about her teenage years though. She's very headstrong and can be very disrespectful when she wants to.

On the other hand, she's extremely loving and compassionate. Her favorite Christmas gift was a ladybug habitat. She "saved" her first ladybug on Christmas day and named her Victoria.

Yesterday, she asked me if she could call her best friend to play. I told her, "Sure. Who should we call?" She answered, "You, Mom!" Yep, she melted my heart.

I've had a good year for the most part. Thank God that my depression over Nick's jaw breaking went away and since my hysterectomy, I feel a ton better too!

My boss has been pressuring me to work more as he wants to fire one of the other hygienists. The issue I have is that he can't keep my schedule full now as it is. I have been told to come in late or leave early too many times to count. He is also pressuring me to go on another work trip, this time to Las Vegas. I am not going, so he makes very rude comments to me.

Who would have imagined that I would become a substitute teacher? I still feel a bit overwhelmed and a part of me wishes that I had never done it. The last-minute calls to work do not sit well with my Type-A personality.

I am in awe of how teachers today work. They not only teach, but they are social workers, and in many cases disciplinarians. The kids in the classrooms have such diverse needs so the teachers need to adjust their lessons to many different levels. In a classroom of twenty or more kids, that is no small feat! I have often come home and prayed. If God could grant me more patience after a day in the classroom, I would be forever grateful.

Nick's job is going well, though he still has no sleep schedule. Couple that with his diagnosis of Severe Obstructive Sleep Apnea with a concern for Aspiration Pneumonia, the poor guy is exhausted. Of course, Dr. Bennett knew it was the tongue all along.

Two "new" vehicles joined our household and two left. We sold my car and Nick's work car to buy me a new car. Nick also bought a 1989 dump truck that we have affectionately named Mater because of the amount of rust on the hood. I love to see how Nick's face lights up over that crazy dump truck. He was excited to be able to plow our dirt road himself this year!

We are looking forward to our Disney trip in the spring. Kenzie and I made a paper chain as a countdown to Disney. Each link signifies a day. She removes one link every day until we leave.

I am dreading my parents' eleven-week trip to Florida, but I am very happy that they can do it. I know they love it there, but I miss them when they're gone.

We welcomed in the New Year with Dean, Tammy, and the kids once again. We played Michigan Rummy for pennies and Collin was the big winner. After midnight, when they were leaving, the poor kid dropped his bag of pennies in the driveway on their way to the car. We all laughed a bit while we helped him pick them all up.

It was nice having Nick home to bring in the New Year with us tonight. Here's to hoping that 2011 is less eventful on the medical end of things!

Monday, July 4, 2011

So far, my wish has been granted and the first half of 2011 has been uneventful. Kenzie enjoyed second grade and I substitute taught quite a bit at her school on the days that I did not work as a dental hygienist.

Nick's jaw has been painful on and off, but he is still holding together, and that is a Godsend! He is enjoying work as well. The comradery among the staff has him laughing a lot and that's great!

We had a fantastic Fourth of July weekend! We camped with my parents at a local campground and our campsites were on the side of the swimming pond. We rode bicycles and went swimming in the pond. Kenzie loves swimming in that pond because it is crystal clear so she can see the turtles and fish swimming near her.

We hiked a 2.5-mile loop at the state forest, played Bingo, and fished in the big pond from our jon boat. When Kenzie caught her first fish of the day, she asked Nick if she could take it off the hook herself. Nick said, "Sure!" with a glimmer in his eye that I don't often see now. Kenzie proceeded to take the fish off the hook and grinned saying, "My life rocks!" I love those family moments!

One night we went out for ice cream sundaes for supper, and today, when we got home, Krista, Gwen, and John came over for a cookout. We had hamburgers and hot dogs, potato salad, macaroni salad, chips, and dessert. Later, we all took a swim and gabbed by the pool.

Tomorrow, I'm making the girls French Toast for breakfast and taking them to the movies. Next week, Kenzie is spending the week at 4H camp's day camp with her friend. She is so excited!

Monday, August 8, 2011

    As our visit to Nick's family approaches, Gloria and I have been spending time on the phone planning meals. Kenzie is very excited to see Eliza, so today she called her to chat.

    When the kids were done talking, I got on the phone with Eliza. I told her that Kenzie is looking forward to seeing her and is so excited. I told her, "You know, you're pretty popular."

    She replied, "I know. Mom's pretty popular too. You know when?"

    "When?" I asked her

    Eliza answered, "She's popular in bed."

    At that point, I almost died laughing. I asked, "What do you mean?"

    She said, "She's popular because I want to sleep with her, the dog wants to sleep with her, and Daddy wants to sleep with her too."

    And just like that, all is right in the world once again.

Monday, August 15, 2001

    The last few days included meeting our great nephew, Jayden, for the first time. Melanie and Joe are absolutely in love with their grandson who they are taking care of for their daughter, Nikki. He's a little sweetheart and at ten months old, he got very comfortable with us right away, which absolutely thrilled me.
    We went to State Fair with Nick's family last Friday and we got to experience chocolate covered bacon. My sister-in-law, Geena, bought fried butter and when she bit into it, it squirted out and ran down her shoulder. She walked around for the rest of the day looking like she had been "blessed" by a bird.
    Today, we drove to one of the biggest water parks in the country and checked into a hotel with Gloria, Nolan, Geena, and Eliza. While we were in the wave pool, Geena got knocked on her bum like a bowling pin when both kids rode the wave right into her legs!
    The water slides there were a blast, and we tried every one of them. By the afternoon, we were ready to relax in the sun for a while.
    Wouldn't you know, a mini cyclone spun up and whipped Geena's sunglasses on top of the hotel roof! It lifted towels and plastic chairs in the air too then dropped them to the ground. It was crazy!
    Geena definitely had a rough time during our visit, but we all had a lot of laughs. As usual, that made it very difficult to leave.

Saturday, September 3, 2011

    We have been without electricity for the last week due to Hurricane Irene. To make matters worse, we have a nine-week-old Cockerpoo puppy that we brought home right after we returned from Gloria's.
    Clyde, our puppy, was a surprise that I had been researching before we left. I have never had a pet, other than fish, ladybugs, and hermit crabs in the house, so I wanted to be cautious with the decision. When we told Kenzie to hurry up and get dressed on the morning after our return, she couldn't understand what the hurry was. She was beyond excited when she met Clyde!
    Clyde is still working on his potty training. The stress of being alone in the dark, while Nick is upstairs sleeping before third shift, and inadvertently stepping in dog pee, or poo, has me on the brink of a nervous breakdown. Couple that with puppy poop in the cracks between our pine floor boards that I need to remove with a plastic knife and a bleach wipe, I am seriously questioning the intelligence of my decision to get Kenzie a puppy.

Friday, November 4, 2011

    Cary and I had our first annual Christmas shopping trip today. We had a ball! We started at 8am and headed to the outlets. We bought the kids a bunch of clothes, then headed to Friendly's for lunch. We then moved on to the malls before a wonderful dinner and a lot of laughs. It was 10pm by the time we got home, but most of our Christmas shopping is done!

    I had been worried about Cary. One of my coworkers told me that she had seen Brandon out at a bar recently. She said that he was in a drunken rage and was yelling and swearing at everyone there. Cary did mention the excessive drinking when we were together today, but thankfully the rage has not made it home to her and her family.

Thursday, December 1, 2011

Two days ago, Nick found pus coming out of an area on his lower left jaw. When he woke up yesterday, he felt lousy and had pain radiating down his neck that lasted all day. He called Dr. Bennett for an appointment.

Dr. Bennett saw Nick today and when he came home, he had an appointment for surgery on December 14th at 7:30 am. He is on antibiotics for the infection until then.

I was so hopeful that we would make it an entire year without a surgery. At least we were close.

Thursday, December 8, 2011

When it rains, it floods…

  This is the second time in the last three months that our basement has flooded. We have been in this house for thirteen years and have never had this happen before.
  Unfortunately, all of Kenzie's Santa gifts were wrapped and hidden in a cardboard box under the cellar stairs. When I sloshed through the four inches of water and pulled the box out, I could have cried. Her *Encyclopedia of Animals* and boxed set of *The Spiderwick Chronicles* were destroyed. Thankfully, her big gift is a basketball hoop and basketball so that was all fine.
  I also had a bag of puppy food down there that broke open. The water swollen food floated all over the basement, under the furnace, under the chest freezer, and in every nook and cranny you could find.
  We spent most of the day cleaning up, except for a trip to Kenzie's pediatrician where she was diagnosed with double pneumonia.

Friday, December 23, 2011

On December 14th, Dr. Bennett removed three screws from Nick's reconstruction plate right in his office. He placed sutures on the inside of Nick's mouth and left the external incision to heal on its own with no sutures or bandage. He told us that the bone looked good, and he gave Nick a pain medication.

Nick has been in extreme pain since the surgery. His blood sugars have been very elevated because of that. When Nick called his physician to ask for a prescription of Humalog, the short acting insulin that he usually needs after every surgery, the doctor covering for his physician refused to call it in.

I called and insisted on speaking with the covering doctor. Once I explained what has been happening to Nick, he finally agreed to call in the prescription.

Today I also drove Nick to Dr. Bennett's office where Dr. Bennett irrigated an area, that was pus-filled, near Nick's most posterior implant.

He took an x-ray and told us that there is a fracture in the same spot that was fractured one and a half years ago. The very same area that he grafted more bone to after that fracture.

Dr. Bennett wants to wait to see if it will heal on its own if Nick doesn't wear his denture and only has liquids. There are screws attached to the bone on either side of the fracture, so he is hopeful that they will stabilize it.

Poor Nick will have another ruined Christmas. He is once again on antibiotics and pain medications. We stopped at the pharmacy on the way home to fill his prescriptions and pick up his Humalog. The covering physician never bothered to call in the needles needed to administer the Humalog. Some doctors are just idiots! Thank goodness we have needles at home from the last time. Their office is now closed for the weekend.

The Next Three Years....

In January 2012, I decided that the writings in my journal would be condensed. I have tended to write only about the experiences that make me happy or make me laugh. I write about the things that I want to remember, or the things that I need to put down on paper to get them off my mind.

The following pages are the highlights of the ups and downs.

2012

This year was one of fantastic family times and stressful health issues. We started out with Nick's broken jaw and his 3D Cone Beam x-ray at a periodontist who I reached out to. The Cone Beam showed that his front implant was drilled through the bone instead of into the bone.

Dr. Bennett, at Nick's next appointment, told us he knew that he had done that and that the Cone Beam was too much radiation. When I told him it was less radiation than the panorex x-ray that he uses, he disagreed.

In April, when my parents returned from Florida, my dad made an appointment with a cardiologist. He had been experiencing dizziness and shortness of breath.

The cardiologist had him wear a halter monitor for forty-eight hours and found that his heart stopped beating for six seconds at a time. They immediately brought him in for surgery to place a pacemaker.

Third grade had caused a lot of stress on Kenzie as she had a teacher who yelled at the entire class instead of the guilty parties. Kenzie was told that she needed to filter out what was meant for her, but when the teacher told the class that they did "Pathetic Math", Kenzie, who got "A"s took it to heart. That and many other teacher comments had Kenzie excited when third grade ended.

By June, Dad's pacemaker became infected and needed to be removed. A new one was placed on the opposite side and is doing fine. Unfortunately, it ruined the vacation plans that my parents had to drive their motorhome out to South Dakota where we would fly to meet them and travel together.

After some quick planning, and a lot of tears in the decision-making process of should we go or shouldn't we, Nick, Kenzie, and I flew to South Dakota on June 21st. Without a doubt, it was the best family vacation that we have ever had. We took in Mount Rushmore, the Bad Lands, Missile Site, Mammoth Site, Wind Cave National Park, Custer State Park, Bear Country, and Deadwood.

We then headed into Wyoming where we visited Devils' Tower, Cody Nite Rodeo, the Buffalo Bill Cody Museum, Yellowstone National Park, and the Grand Tetons. We put over twenty-six hundred miles on the rental car and made tons of memories.

I rode a horse for the first time on a trail ride in Yellowstone. That gave me the courage to allow Kenzie to take horseback riding lessons when we got home. She absolutely loves it!

When we got home, I had M.O.H.S. surgery on my forehead for basal cell carcinoma and got a reminder as to why I shouldn't lay out in the sun. I hope that was my last cancer issue.

In September, we were graced with Hurricane Sandy and in October, poor Gloria fell shortly after and broke her foot. Kenzie also started fourth grade in September and absolutely loves her teacher.

In November, Cary and I went on our second annual Christmas shopping spree. We shopped the outlets then had a late lunch/early dinner at Chelo's. We shopped the malls after that, and I dropped Cary off at home at 10:30pm.

We had a fantastic time and laughed our buns off. She shut my hand in the cargo cover of my car without even noticing. We answered people's questions in unison and were asked if we were sisters, twice. It was a fantastic day!

In the beginning of December, Nick was diagnosed with a torn labrum on his right hip. Thankfully he doesn't need surgery but does need to alter the way he moves. He was also diagnosed with Lyme Disease and was put on antibiotics.

Gloria's visit this year was extra special. I feel like we became even closer friends. I loved our lunch dates and chats. She is irreplaceable!

Kenzie is becoming a very thoughtful young lady. She has always been caring, but now she has really begun to recognize how fortunate she/we are and voices her appreciation frequently. She is always looking for a way to help people and animals and I love that about her.

I would give anything for Nick to be off third shift as he is just not himself when he is sleep deprived. Nonetheless, I feel so blessed to have the husband, daughter, and family I have. I love only working two days a week and volunteering at the school. I never take it for granted and appreciate it greatly.

2013

This year, like most, had its highs and lows. We started our year with a great basketball season for Kenzie. A new tradition was made too! After any game that she made a basket, we took her to our favorite family restaurant for the kid's prime rib.

Unfortunately, January also held tragedies for two families that we care about. One family lost their twenty-year-old son in an auto accident. The other family, who we spent a lot of time with at basketball, had an unexplained health issue. Kenzie's friend Susie's mom started with severe leg pain and ended up with paralysis from the chest down. She was always such a strong, vibrant woman and it was a terrible blow to her and her family.

In February, we drove out to Gloria's for a week with Nick's family. Eliza, Jayden, and Kenzie had a great time sledding and playing together. The adults had a great visit too.

While we were there, Kenzie asked Gloria for a notepad and pen. She was very secretive as to what she was writing, and I couldn't help but have my interest piqued.

When we got home, Kenzie asked to use my computer to type up her "plan". I have to say that what she presented to me later truly surprised me. She wanted to start an after-school club to raise money and awareness for pets, sick kids, and the environment.

Kenzie brought her idea to her teacher, who helped her to set up a meeting with the principal. The principal, unfortunately, did nothing. So, Mrs. Robbins, Kenzie's teacher, asked if I would help her run the Club in her classroom. She is such an awesome teacher!

In March, I went to a dental hygiene continuing education on 3D Cone Beam x-rays. Needless to say, right after that I had all four of my wisdom teeth, and a huge cyst that was deteriorating my jawbone, extracted. For once, this Easter I was the one pureeing my dinner instead of Nick. I had to puree for six weeks to allow for healing so that my jawbone wouldn't break.

In April, Kenzie admitted to being bullied at school since the first grade by one particular student. That girl had hit her in first grade and was taunting her regularly. This year, that girl hit her again and Kenzie decided it was time to tell us. Mrs. Robbins was very supportive and recommended that we invite the school social worker to one of the Club meetings to talk about bullying.

When the Social worker asked the question, "How do you feel when you know you have made someone feel bad?" She told the kids to just think about it, that she didn't need them to answer. I was in complete shock when the bully spoke up and said, "I feel satisfied." My poor kid.

We celebrated Kenzie's tenth birthday in May at the farm where she takes horseback riding lessons. Instead of gifts, she requested pet food that the Club could donate.

Later, Kenzie had five girls sleep over and Nick won their headstand contest for the second year in a row. Kenzie had fun showing her friends her turtle ponds and her new "rescue" turtles, Teddy, Charlie, and Toby. She keeps records on their eating habits and took "DNA" samples and measurements on each.

After Kenzie's birthday, Nick started having jaw pain. It was obvious that something had shifted because his back implant that was being used as a denture rest was no longer under the denture, but on the side of it.

Nick made an appointment with Dr. Bennett, who took a few x-rays and told him that nothing was wrong. He told him to "beat the heck out of the tissue" and call him in two weeks. That man is an idiot! You did not need to be a dental professional to see that something that used to line up doesn't anymore!

In June we saw two months of planning come to fruition. Since January when Susie's mom was paralyzed, our school community had truly come together to support her family. I had set up *Meal Train* so that people could sign up to bring meals to the school five days a week. I then delivered the meals to the family every day.

My sister and I organized bake sales and lolligrams in the spring, but our "Help-A-Friend" fundraiser and walk-a-thon blew us out of the water! We were so fortunate that four well-known companies donated eighty pounds of pasta, six hundred meatballs, huge salads, rolls and butter, and ice cream for the meal. The ice cream company even sent two employees to scoop the ice cream as well as bowls, spoons, and napkins!

Small businesses and local families donated items for a basket drawing and the cafeteria manager donated her time and expertise to organize the serving of food. The school allowed us to use their letterhead when we sent letters to companies, and volunteers helped serve food and clear tables.

When it was over, we were able to hand almost four thousand dollars to our friend and her family from just that fundraiser. We were truly blessed to be able to pull it off.

On Kenzie's last day of fourth grade, she and her classmates celebrated everything they had accomplished since April. In those months, they donated one hundred pounds of dog food and eighty-six pounds of cat food and litter to local animal shelters. The Club donated ten large boxes of books to Harris Children's Hospital and rid two local walking trails of litter. A collection/recycling program for empty juice boxes was started in the classrooms and cafeteria. The Club sent the boxes in and were awarded funds to help the school.

In July, my parents took the trip to South Dakota and Wyoming that they had missed out on last year. We then met up with them in Colorado and did a two-week tour of that state. Some of my favorite spots were the Denver Wildlife Sanctuary, The Royal Gorge Route Railroad, Garden of the Gods, Sand Dune National Park, Mesa Verde, Ouray Hot Springs, Black Canyon of the Gunnison National Park, Colorado National Monument, and the Denver Zoo. While we were there, we were able to connect with some of Nick's cousins too. It was a great trip!

August brought a visit from Gloria! She had originally resisted coming in the summer because she thought that we had a lot of insects at that time of year. We don't, and she was only here two days when she decided that she will have to visit in the summer every year. She made me beyond happy when she fell in love with my pool as that is my happy place and the one place that I truly relax.

Nolan, Geena, and Eliza came to visit the day after Gloria left. We enjoyed the ocean and tubing on the pond with them too. Poor Eliza got wiped out by a wave at the beach and came up screaming. Tough kid that she is, she hopped back in right away.

On Kenzie's first day of fifth grade, her principal asked me to meet with him after school. The news of the Club's successes last school year had reached him, so he asked if I would like to run the Club as an after-school program. Kenzie was beyond excited!

She and I made up a permission slip for the principal's approval and filled out all the necessary forms to use the school. Within two weeks, the Club had thirty members and we were meeting every Thursday after school.

In October, I started my own business making custom woodcrafts and signs. I had been contemplating doing it for the last two years and Gloria finally talked me into taking the leap. I have been very unhappy with my boss and the changes in the office. Dental hygiene has become more about the money than the patient and I don't believe in that.

Substitute teaching was not making me happy either. I had found that many kids are extremely disrespectful to each other and the adults around them. One eighth grader even shoved me. Starting my business has given me a bit of hope that someday I may switch careers entirely, but only time will tell.

In November, we took Kenzie to a Keith Urban and Little Big Town Concert. It was phenomenal! Keith Urban has a great personality and awesome skills, while Little Big Town harmonizes like no one we've ever heard.

We had a wonderful Thanksgiving with our traditional tablecloth signing, then Gloria came on December 17th for the Christmas season.

We had a great visit and Christmas with Gloria. She mixes so well with my family, and she loves the holiday as much as we all do.

We ended the year with Nick wanting Kenzie to take a Hunter's Safety Course. I am dead set against it! I worry enough about him, never mind worrying about my child.

2014

Our year got off to a fantastic start! In January, Nick, Kenzie, and I flew to Florida to spend five days with my parents in their motorhome. We went to Sea World to do their Dolphin Encounter where we fed, touched, and helped to train the dolphins. We also went to Clearwater Marine Aquarium to see Winter and Hope and to Apollo Beach to see the manatees. The weather was great, and we really enjoyed the trip.

Kenzie's Club also had a great start to 2014 with multiple guest speakers. We had an organic gardener, educators on electricity use, an animal control officer, and an environmental protection officer with her search and rescue dog. Watching her dog find Kenzie in her hiding place was a big hit with the kids!

To make things even better, Susie, Kenzie and I delivered twenty boxes of books to the Harris Children's Hospital after our book drive. The Club also collected four hundred and fifty dollars' worth of groceries at our Food Drive for people in need.

In May, Nick had a ruptured eardrum and noticed that his implant/denture rest was loose. He went to Dr. Bennett, who removed the implant in the office without anesthesia, and told Nick that his bone was fine.

Though Kenzie loved her teachers this year, and was thrilled with the Club, she couldn't wait for the school year to be over. She is still being bullied, and now there is another bully on the school bus. I will never understand why people can't just be kind to each other.

Our summer was spent in the pool or on our boat when Nick and I weren't working. My business really picked up this year as I am now selling online.

Kenzie and Gwen hadn't been as close as they used to be, and it made me sad. Krista and John decided to send Gwen to an after-school daycare last fall, so the kids didn't see that much of each other.

This summer though, we have had some fun with Gwen, and it's been awesome! One day in August, Krista, John, and Gwen joined us on the boat for a day of tubing and picnicking. At one point, we pulled up to the beach, I got out of the boat, slipped, and fell under it. Krista said, "Where's Yve? I can hear her, but I can't see her." I yelled, "I'm down here, under the boat!" We laughed our asses off and I got teased quite a bit about it for the rest of this year.

On the Friday of Labor Day weekend, Nick and I picked Kenzie and Gwen up after school and went to a local fair. We visited the animal barns as we always do, and Kenzie fell in love with a little lionhead rabbit. She asked us if she could buy him for herself and I said, "No." At that point, Nick pulled me aside and said, "Do you want to tell her that if she releases her turtles back into the pond, she can get the rabbit? I know how much you don't like the turtles."

BINGO! GREAT IDEA! Kenzie agreed, and on Saturday we went to the pond to release the turtles in the areas that she had found them.

On Labor Day, we picked up her bunny, Hopper, and got him situated in his new home on our front porch. That little bugger is absolutely adorable. You can't help but love him!

In September, school and the Club started up again. I am now in charge of forty-nine students after school every Thursday. My friend, Erica, helps me and offered the use of the library's community room for our meetings.

In October, Nick was in a lot of pain, so he went to see Dr. Bennett. His jaw was broken again. Dr. Bennett was supposed to give him a prescription for pain medication, but he forgot, so I ran around trying to get one from my boss so that we wouldn't need to drive the hour back to Dr. Bennett's. Of course, as was par for the course, they found a questionable area on my mammogram on that same day, and I needed to have more testing.

On October 16, Dad and I took Nick to Harris Hospital for 6:40am for surgery. At 11:30am, Dr. Bennett came out to us to say that he had placed a new titanium plate across the bottom of Nick's jaw and removed a screw from the area that was broken. He did not need to harvest any hip bone. Thank God!

Dad and I were allowed to see Nick at 1pm and by 1:40, they booted him out of the hospital. He was in a lot of pain from the surgery, but more from the intubation. They had tried to intubate him four times before they got it in correctly.

That night, Nick was very nauseous and vomited in the kitchen sink. He thought that he had vomited undigested jello, but it wouldn't dissolve in hot water. It was a whole sink strainer FULL of lubricant from the nasal intubation! My poor hubby. AND, he had to puree again until just before Christmas.

In November, my dad turned seventy, so we celebrated with a surprise party. Cary and I also had our third annual Christmas shopping spree and laughed our buns off after we almost ran out of gas while stuck in traffic.

Gloria had surgery earlier this year, so she only came at Thanksgiving time. We all had missed her so much and really enjoyed having her here to celebrate her eightieth birthday. She was also here when Kenzie was recognized by the Board of Education for the Club and was asked to give them a small presentation on it. We were all very proud of our girl!

The Club did a Holiday Food Drive and donated over five hundred dollars' worth of groceries. They also had a Community Garden over the summer and donated the produce to families in need.

December 20th marked the ten-year anniversary of the accident. Many of our friends reached out to us that day. Kenzie, Nick, and I went out for dinner that night, since Nick had just gotten the okay to chew again. When we got home, we had a message on our answering machine from Brandon, asking how Nick was. It took Brandon ten years to call. When Nick called him back, he didn't answer, nor has Nick heard from him again.

Kyle posted on Facebook that day. He wrote about Nick, without naming him, but told his story and spoke of the man Nick is. I cried when I read it. Kyle is a great guy.

Nick worked six over times that week and wanted to work overtime on Christmas too. That is his way of dealing with things. He just works. Thankfully, after talking, he agreed not to work the Christmas overtime.

You only get one life. Working your way through it instead of enjoying the little things is just living, it's not a life.

On New Year's Eve, as I looked out my bathroom window, there was a button buck standing not ten feet from the house. Nick was in his tree stand on the other side of the property. Sometimes, you just have to laugh.

Deer on a Tote Road

Epilogue

March 2022

    Our lives are so very different now. On April 1st, it will make five years since Nick retired from the Department of Corrections. He spends time year-round doing what he loves, hunting and fishing. He also works for an excavator, breaking his back shoveling, but loving the outdoor work. He has been without another surgery since 2014. Thank the good Lord! His eating is still difficult, and he chokes frequently. He still has pain on a regular basis, especially with weather change. We know that in time, things will break down, but we are thankful for the years without hospital stays.

    In May, it will be six years since I retired from dental hygiene and started to work for myself full-time. My business has grown to be a full-time job and I feel so fortunate to be home doing what I enjoy. I have also written three children's books for daycare and classroom settings as I still absolutely love kids and admire teachers.

    Kenzie left the days of bullying behind in 2016 when she asked me to homeschool her. She had been asking since the first grade, but with my dental hygiene position, it was impossible to do. Once I left that job, she waited six months to broach the subject again and we decided to take the leap.

    I homeschooled Kenzie from seventh grade through high school and watched her develop into a strong, confident woman. She has worked on various farms through the years to earn the money she needs to support her own farm. She started back in 2014 with Hopper and has since added more rabbits, goats, chickens, ducks, geese, sheep, horses, barn cats and a livestock guardian dog.

    We should have seen the farm coming with that little girl's love for animals. She is currently in college working toward a degree in Sustainable Food and Farming, while working and being active in FFA as our State Reporter.

    Gloria passed away two years ago. She was joking with us until the very end. We all miss her tremendously and I still go to pick up the phone to call her at times.

My parents are no longer snowbirds, but still wish to travel. We still spend a lot of time with them, and I am cherishing that.

Cary and I still see each other frequently and share a friendship that I value beyond words. We have supported each other for twenty years and I can't imagine a life without her.

Brandon still keeps his distance, but when I have seen him, I feel comfortable. Nick never sees him, but I am sure he would feel the same. The passage of time heals and though Nick still has many unanswered questions, he is not a grudge bearer.

They say that everything happens for a reason. I am a firm believer in that. Had it not been for that snowy day in December of 2004, my daughter would never have gotten to know and love Gloria the way that she did. Having her here to help those four months was priceless. Nick would also never have gotten the chance to spend time with Kenzie as much as he did when she was very small. They made a lot of memories that they will never forget.

The accident taught me a very valuable lesson. It made me realize that we need to enjoy each other and our lives. We should be willing to try new things and take a chance on making a wrong decision, because it might just be the best decision we have ever made. This woman, who once was a meek, bullied, little girl herself, afraid of animals and her own shadow, is now helping her daughter on a farm and running her own business.

Times have changed, and life, well, life is good.

Deer on a Tote Road

Deer on a Tote Road

Made in United States
North Haven, CT
28 May 2022